i/t   Arthur. J. Silvin.   3/6

15

£5

D1639525

BURKE'S STEERAGE

Burke's Steerage

OR

*The Amateur Gentleman's Introduction to
Noble Sports and Pastimes*

BY

T. H. WHITE

Collins
48 Pall Mall London S.W.1

COLLINS CLEAR-TYPE PRESS : LONDON AND GLASGOW
COPYRIGHT 1938

CONTENTS

PART I

PART II

PART III

CONTENTS

PART I

HUNTING

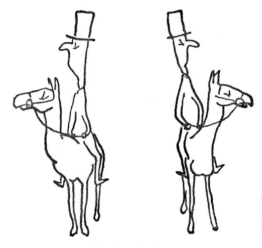

Old Family Pack

§ I

TYPES OF HUNT

THERE are in this island about four main types of hunt, and your first duty as a hunting man will be to decide which type your own hunt belongs to. There are, to begin with, what we may broadly call the *Leicestersheer Hounds*, which hunt the flying grass country of the shires and about whom little can be intimately known by persons of less than cabinet rank, unless by Jewish families with a flair for stockbroking, or by gentlemen of title who may have been benefactors of their race in inventing Night Starvation, Body Odour, Soaps That Wash Two Shades Whiter, Things That Even Your Best Friends Won't Tell You, and preparations for making ladies who have bad complexions marry the blond tennis player in the strip picture after all.

These hounds, although the *Tatler* and the *Sporting and Dramatic* are supposed to have offices at all their principal meets, are not well known to the average run of hunting people. They should be referred to frequently, but the fact remains that they are not and need not be personally visited. Their procedure is twofold, either (as they manifest themselves to the vivid imaginations of sporting writers) to sail along all day over grass fields whose rather low but tricky hedges are "flown" by the horses with scarcely any diminution of speed, or (as they are more liable to appear in real life) to come out to the meet in a leopard skin coat and plenty of make up, carrying in arms the latest baby, dandy dinmont, or other cute pet, there to be photographed by the agents sent down for that purpose and published the following week with a suitably intimate caption. If the second course is preferred, it is not necessary to pay much attention to the hounds (except in being photographed while one of the hounds smells the baby) although it is generally preferable to have one horse. In the latter case, on the days when you are tired of being photographed on foot in the leopard skin coat—with perhaps a neat sling or clean bandage in some visible place—you can sit upon the horse while it walks in a long procession of horses towards the first draw, and you will then be photographed from upside down by one of the fashionable reporters who nest in trees along the lanes frequented by these packs of hounds.

The Leicestersheer hounds are closely associated with the number four. Your horse should cost four hundred guineas, the number of top hats in the average procession should number about four hundred, your subscription should be in the neighbourhood of four hundred pounds, and for all we know there may be four hundred bitches in the kennels. Unless you are a person of title or position (but it rather depends what kind of position—for instance it is no good being the Poet Laureate or some stuffy old scientist with the Order of Merit) you will be well advised to keep away from Leicestersheer, for nobody will consent to take your photograph, and hence all point in coming out will disappear. You will certainly never see the fox, for while you are waiting at the other end of a procession of four hundred horses, the artful creature will probably have run one of his points of four hundred miles, long before you have put your half-crown in the hunt servant's cap and got past the barrage of photographers.

The next main category of hounds may well be called the *Family Pack*. It falls into two sub-divisions, the Old and the Young, but both are characterised by a single peculiarity: an attitude towards strangers of hatred and contempt. The Family Packs are run for the benefit of *residents*, and the Old fear that strangers have come to take their property away from them, while the Young fear that they have come to take away their prestige: that the stranger is going to ride faster than they do. Another reason for hating the stranger, common to both sub-divisions, is that all the residents hate each other so much that they do not want their numbers to be added to, and thus the burden of hatred increased.

The Old Family Pack is supported by the squirearchy over whose land it hunts, a collection of generals, admirals, magistrates, two or three sporting peers, and all the aged aunts and the few unmarriageable daughters that belong to them. Most of these persons

13

are the younger sons of several generations of younger sons of a duke who lived there in 1750. They are all past middle age and pursue the fox because no other course of action has ever occurred to them. If you wish to join their ranks you should buy a property in the neighbourhood and reside there for twenty years, by which time, if he is in a good temper, the hunt secretary, if he is one of these new men, may say Good-Morning to you.

The Young Family Pack is of a type similar to that of its neighbour, but it comes of families whose powers

Young Family Pack

of procreation were more virile. The younger sons of the duke, in this case, are still busy producing younger sons, and the result is that the average age of the field is still reasonably low. With greater youth there goes a greater sexual jealousy, and this is why the Young Family Pack is more concerned about its prestige than its property. If you go there, you will find that it is out to ride against you. It is out, for that matter, to ride against itself; and the hatred extended towards you as a stranger can scarcely be greater than the hatred already existing between the established rivals in the field. This is another contributory cause which keeps the Young Family Pack young: we mean the high mortality occasioned by riding against one another, which soon polishes off all those who are not in the prime of life. In contrast to the Old Family

Pack, with its mulberry coats and rather resigned-looking horses, the Young Family comes out in brand-new scarlet tails with the top hat worn at an angle, and sometimes even an eye-glass screwed into the haggard face with its demon eyes, on bright bay horses which kick one another in sympathy with their masters. The fair neophyte may be warned, in passing, that if she has elected to come out with these hounds her face should be thickly coated with flour, while her lips should be boldly drawn in scarlet vermilion, obtainable at any artist's colour-man or oil shop.

The third pack of hounds to be mentioned in this catalogue may be called *The London Gentleman's* or *Good-Luck-to-All-where-None-are-Known*. Supported entirely by a floating population of stockbrokers, actresses, parvenus, Old Public School Boys, horse copers, and super-salesmen who sell motor-cars in Bond Street, but come down for the meet, there is a singularly happy atmosphere to be met with in this field. Since everybody is a perfect stranger to everybody else, nobody knows but what you may be a local duke or even the master of the hounds, and the result is that great courtesy is extended in all directions. Persons converse with one another freely at the covert side, each attempting to augment the other's supposition that each is a person of distinction who has hunted before. Few of them have, in fact, hunted before, but all of them have read books about it, and the result is that they take hunting seriously, chattering away about Pelhams and snaffles with great care to use the words correctly, and chaffing one another in the most knowing and bonhommous way about falls and port wine and terrible leaps, just as people are supposed to do in books. The Amateur Gentleman who elects to follow these hounds need have no fears about his

behaviour—so long as he has read, say, Mr. Cecil
Aldin's *Ratcatcher to Scarlet*—because, even if he does
commit a misdemeanour, none of the people who saw
it on Monday will be there to bring it up against him
on Friday. In fact, this is probably the jolliest hunt
that you can possibly belong to, combining, as it does,
a cheerful desire to follow the fox (unlike the lady in
the leopard skin coat) with none of the scowls which
you will get from the Family Pack whether you fall
off your horse or stay on it. But be careful to speak
in a belittling manner about the London Gentleman's,
however much you may have enjoyed it, if you happen
to get a day with the Family or in Leicestersheer.

Our last category need scarcely be mentioned among
serious people. Relegated to some forest of Wales or
crag in Scotland or English stretch of tidal estuary,
the *God-Forsaken* hounds, more harrier than foxhound,
pursue their tedious and forgotten existence in the face
of hardship and disgrace. Nobody goes out with them,
or nobody that is anybody—only farmers and low
people like that. They have never seen a photographer,
probably do not even know that the camera has been
invented. The Master, a man soured by his inability
to get a pack in Leicestersheer, flogs his weary mongrels
across the bogs, corries, slums, mountains, jungles,
marshes, electric railway lines, lagoons and atolls of
his territory, inspired by no other idea than the vulgar
and unfashionable objective of catching foxes.

Taxing Intelligence of Landed Gentry

§ 2

REASONS FOR HUNTING

WHAT, the Amateur Gentleman may now be asking himself, can be the interesting reason which drags such a diversity of types as has been outlined above into the pursuit of this noble and ancient sport of foxhunting? The answer is a curious one, for there exists a wide though unsuspected gap between the real and apparent objectives of this amusing pastime.

The apparent object of foxhunting is to kill wild foxes by means of dogs which have been trained for that purpose by a gentleman who finds it expedient to follow and assist their operations upon the back of a horse. It is nowadays unexpectedly difficult to make a horse follow the hounds in a direct line across the English countryside, it has always been difficult to control the movements and concentrate the attention of such a large body of dogs, and the tricks of so vigilant an animal as our English Reynard are enough to tax the mental ingenuity of almost any of our landed aristocracy. Thus, for the actual huntsmen and those of his immediate entourage actively concerned in operations, the difficulties of foxhunting— the tireless patience and cunning necessary in teaching the hounds, the interest of their management and well-being all through those long summer months when everybody has forgotten about them, the obstacles which make complicated their pursuit and control during the hunting season, and the skill and foresight which have to be matched against the skill and foresight of the fox—these make up the genuine fascination of the chase, a joy which will always repay any triumph over difficulty. For the master, the huntsman, and two whips, the Sport of Kings is probably kingly. But, unfortunately, these four persons are the only ones, even out of the Leicestersheer four hundred, who are really hunting.

What, we may be asked, of the other three hundred and ninety-six? None of these persons is allowed to navigate the pack, to breed or enter the young hounds, to nourish them during the summer months, except as puppies, nor to outwit the fox. For them only one of the difficulties is allowed to remain as a personal interest, and that is the difficulty of riding the horse across country in pursuit of the master, in a kind of pink paper chase. For these persons, in fact, the dangerous part of the proceedings is the only part left, because all the rewarding parts of hunting skill and triumph over hunting difficulty are reserved for the huntsman and his men. About two per centum of these persons actually enjoy the dangerous difficulty of riding straight. For them the triumph over the fence or over the pusillanimity of their timorous quadruped is a genuine joy.

So now there are eight more, out of our Leicestersheer field, who are enjoying their hunting for a direct reason. The huntsman rides to hunt, and these eight are hunting to ride, but all of them are deriving a genuine pleasure which could only be supplied in its peculiar entirety by foxhunting.

There remains three hundred and eighty-eight souls, take them for all in all, and the question is: What is the real reason for their appearance in the field? The answer, we repeat, is a curious one.

At some remote period in the history of foxhunting it was discovered that a field larger than eight was a practical necessity. Not only was a larger number of persons of use in holding up cubs at the beginning of the season, and in providing a complacent audience to applaud and publish the ingenuity of the Master and his huntsmen in their trade, but also the increasing distribution of wealth among the poorer classes had begun to impoverish the owners of hounds so that they could scarcely any longer afford to bear the whole expenditure necessary to a hunting establishment. A subscription was the obvious solution, and the more subscribers there were, the more champagne the Master would be able to buy himself out of the subscription. Accordingly in 1803 a famous Master of one of the Leicestersheer packs consulted the psychologist Pavlov, then a young man of 87, and was informed that the mainspring of all human activity lay in fear. He brought the eminent gentleman back from Russia at his own expense, and a press campaign was immediately set on foot in order to enhance the number of subscribers on this basis.

It was laid down as a preliminary step that fox-hunting was the exclusive recreation of the brave, and at once all those persons who rightly harboured doubts of their own valour sought to convince themselves and the world that these doubts were without cause. Terrified of being terrified, all the spiritual brothers and sisters of the unfortunate Mytton hurled themselves into the hunting field to prove that they were not afraid. But the ingenious Pavlov had not exhausted his invention. It was now announced, as a

Tortured by Uncertainty

coup de grâce, that foxhunting was also the exclusive prerogative of the nobly born. There had been many in those virile days, when the militia was so frequently called out to restore order in the public schools, who were genuinely intrepid and for whom the first threat —a direct fear for their courage—had been without menace. But all of these succumbed to the second. Was their blood, they asked themselves, truly blue and which drawer did it come out of? Tortured by the uncertainty, terrified by the social stigma which would arise out of a continued abstention, they all trooped off to Bond Street to buy themselves top hats.

Their descendants, three hundred and eighty-eight out of that Leicestersheer four hundred, are still hunting, and for the same reasons. Hag-ridden by these terrible doubts, ladies of kindly temperament who would otherwise be plotting dinners with their cooks drag their weary bones out of bed at unearthly hours, dip their faces in the flour bag, and bounce off on horses which bump them underneath, to the unending paper chase. Nervously cutting themselves as they shave, and far too qualmish to eat their porridge, unoffending gentlemen who might otherwise be collecting stamps clamber upon the backs of ill-tempered chestnuts and go out to their purgation of criticism and hate.

Unfortunate Amateur Gentleman, consult with yourself before it is too late to draw back, and ask yourself why you are desirous to hunt. Is it of your virility or of your social status that you entertain such doubts? Hunting, you will find, is an illusory panacea: for the true cure for the former would be to have a handsome wife and a large family, while you can always consolidate the latter by becoming the proprietor of a yellow newspaper and getting a peerage.

§3

HOW TO DRESS

BUT it is useless to expostulate. If you were sensible you would lay aside this book and take to gardening, if you were middle-aged you would nod your head, and sigh, and continue to read. But you are neither sensible, nor middle-aged, and we shall simply have to do the best we can for you. You are a young man, Amateur Gentleman, a subaltern, perhaps, with all your manhood yet to prove. You have yet to learn that the leg which you broke that time in wire will still give you a rheumaticky twinge or two when, as quite an old man, you are wading the Wye in February: have yet to feel your bones cracking as you hack home fifteen miles in the rain after a dull meet: have never yet hurt yourself properly, nor felt that humiliating twinge of satisfaction when the Master decides not to hunt on a slippery day with the mist showing less than half a field. In fact, you are not old enough for salvation, and all that we can do is to make your disillusioning path as comfortable as possible.

Man never looks so noble as when he is raised an extra five feet from the ground and dressed in red. Even the top hat is calculated to lend stature to his dignity, and perhaps the real reason why you are taking to hunting is because you are thus allowed so nobly and so arrestingly to dress up and to assert your manhood. We shall be wise, then, to begin by explaining to you about your clothes.

There are three kinds of fancy dress correctly worn in the hunting field. The first, a prerogative of great age, unassailable social position, heavy powers of subscription, or enormous personal courage, is the full fig. It consists, starting from the top and working downwards, of a hunting top hat preferably without a guard cord—the hunting hat is specially strengthened and has a little leather bag to fall into, so it is no good wearing the one you bought for funerals: a white stock, preferably of silk, with a simple gold pin; a red coat cut either in tails, if you are proud of your thighs, or in the full skirt if you prefer to keep them dry in January; a yellow waistcoat; white breeches, which will require a large staff to keep them clean; black boots with pinkish or mahogany tops; spurs worn the right way up—the right way is the one which appears to be the wrong one; and white, yellow or coloured string gloves.

The second costume, which may be worn by any reasonable subscriber as soon as he has allayed the fears of his new companions by one or two modest appearances in a rat-catcher, is identical with the first, except that the coat is black instead of red and the breeches may be of any shade. If the breeches are white, as sometimes happens when it is a tail-coat, then the boots must still have tops. If they are of any other shade, from khaki to deep brown, then the boots should be "butcher" boots, without tops. In the latter case, a bowler hat is sometimes worn instead of the topper.

The third costume is known as a rat-catcher. This consists of bowler hat, stock, tweed or check coat split up the back, coloured breeches, string gloves and butcher boots. It is worn by minors, the sons of farmers, unassuming people, some horse copers, and by everybody during cub-hunting—except that the stock is replaced by a tie until very late in the season, and the bowler hat by almost anything that comes to hand.

We all know that in taking up hunting one of your principal objects was to wear a red coat, but such are the tortuous workings of the human mind that for some reason we shall be inclined to despise you if you do so at once. The explanation, such as it is, runs something like this: the full fig is worn by the *bona fide* hunting man as an irrefutable assertion or outward and visible sign of his inward and spiritual grace. It signifies in a symbolical manner the following assertion: "I am a true member of the field—*i.e.* (see above) I am brave and nobly born—and I have enough horses to do the thing in style, and I know how to remain in the correct (*i.e.* mounted) position on these horses, and I have enough experience not to disgrace myself, and I can look the hunt secretary in the face or call him by his Christian name because I have paid my generous subscription." If you can lay your hand upon your heart and make this assertion, then you have every right to wear the symbol of it, and nobody will think the worse of you if you appear in red—never mind whether it ought to be called pink—at your very first appearance with any pack of hounds. But consider the other side of the picture. Have you paid a generous subscription? Are you sure that you will not go riding over seeds? Do you invariably retain the mounted position? Is your stable confined to one aged grey and he with a stringhalt? Are you of an intrepid temperament and able to command all the aitches with which nature has endowed the true blue gentleman? How do you expect to look, in your scarlet coat, when, having urged your single grey and prancing steed across a field of sprouting oats, you have timidly compelled him to refuse the small fence at the end of it, and fallen off at the feet of the secretary who still awaits your mean subscription, exclaiming, "O 'ell"? Obviously these feats had better be performed in some unassuming garb which makes no assertion. If you do them in a rat-catcher, your companions will at worst regard you as a harmless imbecile or unfortunate, and they may even think it rather brave of you to continue cheerfully and unassumingly in their performance: but if you do them in the full regalia there is only one epithet left suitable for them to apply, and that epithet of Hypocrite will be richly earned.

What then, O Amateur Gentleman, are your equestrian, financial, hunting and nervous powers? If you are poor, or vulgar, or frightened, or very young, or liable to fall off, believe us that it would be better at present to hide your light under a bushel. Take the sincere advice of those who at one time or another have found themselves in all these dilemmas, and hunt for your first season in a rat-catcher invariably. There is plenty of time ahead of you, time which you will enjoy much more than you do now, however difficult it may be to believe that fact. When you are braver (but it must be admitted that if you are young you will only get less brave—or more sensible) and older than twenty-one and able to avoid the damning charges of poverty and social climbing, then you may well move into a top hat and black coat. When you are known in the county you can go into pink. Meanwhile, be sensible; and remember that it was the person who sat down at the bottom of the table who had the snobbish satisfaction of being asked to go up higher.

There are several small points which are apt to baffle the Amateur Gentleman who is anxious to do the correct thing. We shall attempt to give in this chapter a confused catalogue of little matters which have proved of interest in such cases.

Spurs are a fruitful source of confusion. The truly modest man whose equestrian powers are only partially developed, will, in the first place, refrain from wearing spurs at all. They are a contradictory means of holding on to a horse that is running away, because they are all too liable to make him run the faster. With a nervous or highly strung horse, in the hands of an amateur, they are apt to encourage a velocity or impetuosity undesirable in such circumstances. They look so nice, however, and can even sometimes be encouraged to make a slight jingling noise, that few can be persuaded to do without them. If you must have them, at any rate see that the rowels are filed off. The alteration can rarely be detected, and both yourself and your mount will be spared much needless suffering. They should be attached so that the buckles are on the outside of the foot and the knob of the spur pointing downwards. In walking downstairs with spurs on, it is advisable to walk like a duck; but in general it is best to walk as little as possible in spurs, since the present fashion of wearing them high on the ankle must always result in excruciating agony to the ankle itself. If you leave your horse and have to walk home with him, you had better remove your spurs and hang them on the crossed stirrups, or else you can console yourself with the old motto: *Il faut souffrir pour être belle.*

Another strap which causes confusion is the leg strap at the top of the boot. This should be passed

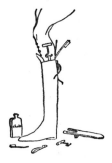

Liberal Use of Shoehorns

through the tag at the back of the boot, and round your own leg below the knee, so that the spare end beyond the buckle when fastened sticks *outwards*. But the whole question of boots is an absorbing one. Their success or failure depends entirely upon the structure of the leg itself. Some legs—the more muscular ones or those with a high instep—are impossible to fit with the true beauty, a beauty which depends upon the tight fit of the top of the boot. For people afflicted with muscular legs we can only suggest the following palliatives: silk socks, breeches which at all costs must button well below the calf, French chalk, and the liberal use of shoehorns and disused toothbrushes for poking the odd folds of flesh and breeches down inside the tops.

A really beautifully kept boot should be as pliable as a stocking. This desideratum can be attained by purchasing half a pint of castor oil at the end of the season and by applying all of it to the boots inside and out. A groom should then be hired at the beginning of June and provided with brushes, *Wren's* boot polish (it is needlessly cruel to use the old-fashioned blacking and spittle) and mutton bones. If he is kept constantly at work, except on Sundays, the castor oil will begin to have worked out by the beginning of the next hunting season in November, and there may be some chance of a shine. You must be very careful what boot polish you use[1]—those that give the best shine most quickly usually do the worst damage—and you must see to it that the boots are never dried before a fire. If you can afford the experiment it will be instructive to dry one pair in such a manner. The startling sensation of putting your foot straight through a pair of boots, as if you were a clown jumping through a paper hoop at the circus, is worth a small outlay.

The fit of the breeches round the knee is not only elegant but necessary. The better the fit at this point, the greater your comfort will be. While we are upon the subject of comfort and the lower man, it may be expedient to make a minor digression into a part of the hunting costume which gives little or no opportunity for display. A pair of pants, or underpants as the Americans are said to call them, is not, it is true, so fruitful a source of satisfaction as a scarlet coat:

---

[1]It is sometimes well to remember how much polish was used, before you cross your knees in front of the fire after breakfast.

but it can cause much hidden sorrow. Do not, unless you have the skin of a rhinoceros, wear short pants. They have a way of rumpling up and causing the most painful sores half-way down the inside of the upper leg. Wear long pants and remember to hitch them over your braces, unless you want them to come down inside your breeches and add to the discomforts of your seat.

Your waistcoat need not in all the fancy dresses be plain yellow. A certain amount of latitude—your tailor will explain to you how much—is allowed in this garment, and it is always pleasant to have a little personality. Keep your half-crowns in its pockets, where they will be more accessible than in other recesses, unless you have a watch pocket outside your coat.

The paper packet which contains your stock when you buy it will probably have some pictures explaining how it should be tied. These pictures will not, however, add the further information that it is unlikely to retain its position unless you make use of two safety-pins thus:

Stocks and gloves, like dress ties and shirts, can only be worn once before sending them to the wash. The laundry will then unravel the gloves and you can buy yourself some new ones.

The delicate question of hunt buttons is treated so variously in different hunts that the only safe advice is this: wear plain brass buttons on a red coat or plain black buttons on a black one, until somebody urges you to do something else.

The hunting top hat is, in its way, almost as interesting as the boot.

It is subject to the same vicissitudes. When it is new, it is beautiful: when it has been through a few blackthorns and received a dent or two from a tree as you were jumping under it, it begins to be a problem. Some Gentlemen's gentlemen attempt to retain its gloss by an initial dressing of beer or glue size. The latter stratagem renders it impervious to its furry weals, but removes much of its deep lustre. You will probably be able to make it look moderately all right by stroking it with the hands after the application of water, but, if not, you had better pretend to yourself that it was in good condition at your setting forth that morning, until you happened to ride under a tree or rumpled it in the car. It is surprising how well you can make other hunting people believe things, if you can only contrive to believe in them yourself.

There remain a few accessories which cannot properly be called dress. Get a good heavy hunting crop—not the lady's size, unless, of course, you happen to be a lady—and carry it in the right hand with the bone handle downwards. Use it to open gates, when it will be most useful, so long as you remember to change it to your left hand when opening a gate which swings to the left. If you pursue the opposite tactic you will set yourself a puzzle which can only be solved by jumping over the crop.

Your saddle will have a couple of little rings for carrying a sandwich-case, unless you prefer to take a small packet of biscuits and chocolate in your pocket, and a leather cigar-case may give comfort on the way home. Many people prefer not to take metal cases in their pockets, having a fanciful objection to being rolled on their sharp edges by horses if they happen to be rolling about. For the same reason a wrist-watch, rather than a pocket watch, is useful for telling you the time at which you may safely go home, without incurring the reputation of being a coward.

The last accessory, a flask of drink, raises a vexed question. It must be plainly understood that the three hundred and eighty-eight persons, who have been driven by fear into the Leicestersheer field, have encountered in that field another series of fears equally intimidating. They hunt because they fear for their courage and gentility, and while they are hunting they very naturally fear for their bones. In this dilemma there is little left for them to do, except to deaden their feelings with drink. A large flask has been designed for this emergency, which fits into a kind of leather telescope case that can be attached to the saddle. It is carried quite openly by followers of the London Gentleman's (who like their little drop of tiddly in any case) but some of the Family Packs consider it too open a confession of weakness, and we must therefore regretfully conclude that it is not nowadays considered exactly smart.

Meditating on God's Providence

§4

PURCHASE AND HIRE OF HORSES

THE Amateur Gentleman may as well make up his mind at once that it is impossible to buy a horse without being swindled. Being an amateur he will almost certainly know nothing about horses, whose lore requires a long and painful schooling, and hence it will be impossible for him to go out among the farms to choose a likely young horse upon his own initiative. Nor, unless he intimately knows the character of a groom who has served his family for fifty years, will it be safe for him to relegate the task to other hands. Few grooms can be relied upon to be so stupid that they would not accept a 50 per cent commission from the vendor and then double the purchase price.

Unable to purchase direct from the producer, except by trusting himself quite blindly to chance, the future owner will be thrust upon the mercies of the dealer who sells the made horse at six years old. This animal has no fixed value. The same horse purchased from Mr. A., who keeps the depressed livery and bait stable behind the mews, will be worth £70—he came from the farmer at twenty-five—where he would be worth £150 from Mr. B., who farms his own land and often hires out horses for the hunt servants in times of crisis, or £250 from Captain C., who runs the impressive stables just outside of Leicestersheer and has little trees in green barrels before the door of every loose-box.

Confronted by this seemingly impenetrable problem we consulted the least disreputable dealer known to us, and he swore the following affidavit before a commissioner for oaths: "I am a man of small wit and limited perceptions, and I have never felt a horse's legs in my life. I have always refrained from this action because I do not know what I ought to be feeling for, and I am convinced that any alert groom would immediately detect my ignorance if I began to fumble. My knowledge of horses is limited to the following simple definition: A horse should have a head, a body and four legs, all made of the same material. The mane and tail are optional. Apart from wooden legs and other very rare afflictions, it is subject to six main ailments which are readily detected by the naked eye. These are: absence of one or both eyes, a sort of round plug-hole in the middle of the throat, inability to stand up without support, ewe neck, capped hocks, and a tendency to scratch the stomach with the hind hoofs when walking. I never remark upon these defects and am not particularly interested in their occurrence. My method of purchase depends upon a single talent, the faculty for deep and unbroken silence combined with complete inertia.

"When I visit a stable for the purchase of horses I signify my wants in as few words as possible and ask that the suitable mounts should be led out for my inspection. Upon a horse being brought before me, I station myself directly in front of it, with my hands behind my back, and look at its ears. With my eyes fixed upon these organs I meditate upon God's providence in providing us with a sense of hearing. After some time I remove my gaze to its eyes, reflecting upon the blessing of sight and upon the delicacy of those miraculous nerves which somehow convey a message from the retina to the brain. I thus slowly pass downwards, joint by joint, until, with the hoofs, I am pondering the mysteries of locomotion; and then I move on to the left side of the animal, where I repeat the exercise. After I have examined him from both ends and from both sides, I signify by a wave of the hand that he may be led away and another animal substituted for my inspection. It is important that no inquiry about his price should be made at this stage.

"When all the available horses have been paraded, or all for which we have time during this somewhat lengthy process, I select either the even or the odd numbers at random, and cause them to be brought out one by one once more. I now signify by signs that the grooms should cause the creature to walk and run before me, up and down the stable yard. This soon takes the fire out of a groom, breaks down his natural resilience and renders his usually poker face perfectly transparent.

"At the third stage I again select the odd numbers of the odd numbers, or the even of the even, and by this means am generally left with about three mounts. I now repeat both the first stages with each of these horses, with this difference, that after each inspection of each point of the horse I inspect and meditate upon the corresponding point in the dealer. When you have stared for five minutes at the capped hocks of a horse, and then gone round in silence to stare at the hocks of the dealer, the man will be ready to break down without further prompting and to exclaim that capped hocks are only a blemish of appearance. I make no reply.

"Having selected out of the last three the animal which has called forth the fewest pleas and excuses during my inspection of its owner, I call in a veterinary surgeon resident in my own district, and, if he is prepared to certify the creature, I open my mouth for the first time in inquiring the price. I deduct two-thirds from the figure stated, and invariably take the animal home at once; very often with a stiff double whisky thrown in free by the vendor, who is profoundly grateful to me because I am going away and generally in need of some strong stimulant himself."

This advice, sound as it is, can unfortunately be of little use to the amateur, lacking, as he will do, the stamina and world-wide reputation of the authority who gave it. If, therefore, an alternative is required, we would suggest that there are only two safe ways of buying a horse. The one is, if you can afford to pay through the nose, to patronise some very famous dealer who has his own reputation to consider; the other, to entrust the whole matter to a learned and intimate friend. In the case of dealers and veterinary surgeons, let them be as much as possible men who live locally in the hunt you intend to patronise, for such people will probably prefer not to soil their own doorsteps.

On the whole, then, it is safer to begin your hunting career by hiring horses rather than by buying them. You can always end by buying a horse that you have begun by hiring, if he happens to suit you particularly well.

The smallest amount of rational inquiry among local people will put you in possession of the names of persons who let out hirelings in the district which you intend to hunt. A few further questions and a little discrimination will tell you which of these establishments is the best. Go to this establishment and, after asking for the proprietor and viewing his horses, ask him his terms. These will not be less than two guineas a day, and need not in the average case be a great deal more. It is advisable to ask at once whether this includes the navigation, by a groom, to and/or from the meet.

At this point the Amateur Gentleman will be well advised if he will consent to consider a gentle admonition. During the early stages of his hunting career every amateur must find himself confronting situations of which he has neither cognizance nor control, even after closely following this terse and invaluable book. These situations will only humiliate him if he has pretended to greater experience than he actually possesses. What is more, many of them would not have arisen if he had not indulged in that pretence. What is perhaps even more than that, it is highly improbable that any such pretence will deceive anybody who has had anything to do with horses.

In interviewing the riding master of the present instance, there will be an almost irresistible desire to pose as an experienced horseman and rider to hounds, a desire which should be combated with every means in one's power. If, by some extraordinary miscarriage of justice, you should contrive by accident to carry off the deceit, you will find that you have laid up for yourself nothing but trouble and sorrow. Your first slip will become not a mistake, but an exposure and a humiliation, while it will be liable to come more quickly. Supposing you to be a person of some skill, the proprietor of the hirelings may mount you on one of his less amenable charges, or on one whose tenderness of mouth, in conjunction with your own tendency to maintain your equilibrium by means of the reins, can only result in scenes of a ridiculous if not a dangerous character.

Far better, then, to confront the fellow in a manly way and to say to him:

"I have $\begin{Bmatrix} \text{seldom}^1 \\ \text{never} \end{Bmatrix}$ hunted before, but $\begin{Bmatrix} \text{I have been to} \\ \text{I used to ride} \end{Bmatrix}$
Mr. So-and-So's riding school for a fortnight^1 a donkey when my parents lived in India $\Big\}$ and I
want a $\begin{Bmatrix} \text{broken down}^1 \\ \text{slow but sure} \\ \text{experienced} \end{Bmatrix}$ horse which will carry me
safely and give me a reasonable glimpse of the such-and-such hounds on such and such a date."

¹Strike out the words that are not applicable.

The man will be far more impressed by your obvious grasp of the situation than he would be by any pretences—which could only denote a failure to grasp the situation—and he will serve you fairly, carefully and honestly in consequence.

Ridiculous if not Dangerous

How to Cap

§ 5

A SMALL MATTER OF SUBSCRIPTIONS

You have bought yourself the correct uniform and provided yourself with a horse which, it is to be hoped, will behave as correctly, and now you will be wondering whom else you have got to pay for what.

If you can borrow a copy of Bailey's Hunting Directory, you will find that the hunt which you intend to patronise lays down a definite scale of charges, with the alternatives of paying £2 a day (or perhaps £3 on the days when the hounds are in their best country) or of making an inclusive subscription of about £25 for one day a week during the season.

The daily charge is invariable, but the seasonal subscription is allowed to vary a great deal among *persons resident in the county*. When it is obvious to all that you are a gentleman of small means living in reduced circumstances, the hunt secretary will generously accept whatever subscription you feel capable of offering, and this for two reasons. First, he knows that in point of legal fact no charge can be made—if you choose to follow the hounds without any payment whatever, the master will have no means of redress except to disoblige all the other members of the field, as well as yourself, by taking his hounds home. Secondly, the hunt secretary knows that you know that a detailed balance sheet will probably be issued to subscribers at the end of the season, in which booklet your name and subscription will be published to your neighbours. This he has found by experience to be a great deterrent to meanness.

For persons resident in the county, therefore, the terms laid down in Bailey are little more than a guide. The residents are supposed to subscribe on the principle that they will give as much as they can possibly afford.

This supposition, as a close examination of the booklet in question would prove to you if you could lay hands on it, is only partly true. The actual principle is that residents with a strong sense of security or personal value content themselves with the Bailey subscription as a maximum—and sometimes with a great deal less—while those whose means or social status are on a dubious level strive to reassure themselves with a heavier subscription. Look closely and you will see that poor Mr. Jones, who drives about in a 1928 Morris Oxford, has given his thirty guineas, while Captain the Hon. "Piggy" Plantaganet, who keeps six horses and has champagne for dinner every night, has contented himself with a subscription of fifty pounds.

The Amateur Gentleman who has reflected upon these phenomena, and examined his own bank balance, will now be in a position to decide upon his own course of action. He will ask himself first of all whether he proposes to hunt on more than twelve and a half woodland days or eight and one-third days over grass. Should he be a business gentleman with only one horse, or a gentleman more than usually subject to the influenza and other winter accidents, he may decide that he cannot be sure of more than twelve hunting days and that therefore it will be cheaper to stump up day by day. In this case he will simply ride out to his first meet without further ado, carrying in his pocket two (or three) pound notes and half a crown for the wire fund. Almost before he knows where he is, a contemptuous, bilious, but ingratiating gentleman will range a horse alongside of his own, raise his top hat in a perfunctory gesture, and inquire whether he is a subscriber to these hounds? Blushing furiously, as if detected in a felony, the Amateur Gentleman will now mumble out whatever phrases may occur to his disordered mind, and hand over the pound notes as if he were attempting to dispose of stolen property. On subsequent occasions, when he knows the hunt secretary by sight, he can save himself much of this suffering by riding up to the gentleman in question on his own initiative, the moment he sees him, and making a clean breast of it before he is apprehended.

Should the humble reader, on the other hand, be a resident in the county, or a weekly visitor from London whose youth and sanguine temperament make

it unlikely that he will be incapacitated by the influenza
for more than half of the hunting season, he will
probably decide to become a full-fledged subscriber.
He will therefore write to the hunt secretary, several
days before his first appearance in the field, stating
that he hopes to have the pleasure of following his
lordship's hounds during the coming season and that
he encloses a cheque for such-and-such an amount in
respect of so many horses. If rich, he may as well add
a little to the sum laid down in Bailey; if not rich,
he had better begin by sending the full Bailey sum (he
can always reduce it next season); and if poor he will
have to recast the entire letter, stating that he, a
resident, hopes the hunt secretary will be able to accept
of whatever disgraced figure he is in a position to offer,
in consideration of his good intentions and earnest
desire to increase the subscription as soon as his own
finances are on a more prosperous footing.

These preliminaries having been accomplished, the
Amateur Gentleman can go out to his first meet with
an easy conscience. The hunt secretary will waylay
him as usual, and ask the usual question. The Amateur
Gentleman will proudly reply, "I sent you a small
subscription last Thursday." If he leaves it at this he
will have made a false step, for the hunt secretary,
though vaguely conscious of having received some
such communication, will neither have troubled to
answer the letter nor to remember the name of the
outsider who sent it. He will therefore feel at a disad-
vantage and dislike the Amateur Gentleman from the
start. But if the Amateur proceeds at once to state his
name and address in a humble manner, all may yet
be well. The secretary will then introduce him to the
master (a man very reasonably preoccupied with the
management of so many dogs and emulous though

terrified people, and one, therefore, who will be grateful if you relieve him of the burden of your company after the briefest interchange of pleasantries) and in due course you will receive a copy of the hunt booklet, at the end of the financial year, with your initials wrongly reported, your address confused, and your subscription under-estimated by several pounds.

Master Conversing Amiably

Pavlov's Famous Code

§ 6

CONDUCT IN THE HUNTING FIELD

THE psychologist Pavlov had not completed his deadly work when he laid down his two great maxims. What he had already done was sufficient to draw the people *into* the hunting field, but it was now expedient that he should invent some way of keeping them there. Paid as he was with a handsome salary by the M.F.H. who had imported him from Russia, the elderly gentleman sat down in a tower room which is still shown to visitors, and there elaborated his famous hunting code.

Pavlov's code was based upon the same simple hypothesis which had dictated his maxims: that all human conduct is motivated by fear. He had frightened the upper classes into the hunting field and he must keep them there by the same means. In this he was of course very largely assisted by the fortunate circumstance that a certain amount of physical danger does naturally accompany the elevation of heavy bodies, by muscular action, above the surface of the earth to which in normal circumstances the forces of gravity would keep them contiguous. He was uncertain, however, that mere physical danger would be sufficient for his purpose, or indeed that there was enough of it to be really noticeable in the hunting field. He therefore decided to supplement Nature by the addition of certain spiritual dangers of an artificial kind. These were to be the terrible, since intangible, dangers of mental uncertainty.

Pavlov's first step was based upon his observation of secret societies in his native land and of the conduct of children at preparatory schools in our own country. In both instances, and also in some Polynesian taboos, he had observed the incidence of a secret language which served to give the ring-leaders a feeling of superiority and to terrify the uninitiate. He invented, therefore, an arbitrary language for foxhunters in which dogs were called hounds (but always without the definite article); tails, brushes; feet, pads; heads, masks; whips, crops; red, pink; and countless other curiosities of diction.

It was a sound step, but only a preliminary one, for it soon became obvious that the language could be learned with a little patience. The uninitiate readily became initiated, and thus, since there was nobody to terrify, the feeling of superiority itself evaporated.

But Pavlov was not at a loss. As soon as the ramifications of the secret language had begun to sink into the unconscious of his victims, the unscrupulous scientist countermanded all its rules. Red was not pink, but pink red. Ruthless amidst the terrors of the general upheaval, he proceeded to strike and strike again while the iron was still hot. Red was not pink, but scarlet: scarlet was not pink but red. Bulls and protocols issued daily from the tower room, all of equal validity, all contradictory, and none were countermanded. With the world of phenomena and noumena reeling about them, the hunting aristocracy staggered from meet to meet, never quite certain whether the hounds were the hounds, or merely hounds. An internal feeling of jealousy and suspicion quickly sprang up. Somebody had distinctly heard the master talking of dogs (but was he being jocular?) while somebody else was sure that Lady Industrial Revolution had been wearing a veil with a bowler, or a topper without a veil, they were not quite sure which.

For the campaign had by now been carried from the world of ideas to the world of objects. Which way up did one carry one's crop, and was it a crop or a whip? Which way up were one's spurs, one's stock (or cravat?), one's self? Terrorized by the obvious danger of being the wrong way up, the upper classes —they hoped that they were still upper—could, after a few agonizing weeks, never again afford to leave the stricken field, for fear that its values should alter in their absence.

It is to a society still flinching under the hammer blows of a Russian's diabolic ingenuity that it is now our task to introduce the Amateur Gentleman. He is to go out into a congeries of three hundred and eighty-eight persons, men, women and young children, all justifiably suspicious that if they tumble off their horses the ground will give them a bump, all mutually antagonistic for fear that they are not (*a*) brave; (*b*) blue blooded; (*c*) the right way up, and all, in some fields, in advanced stages of intoxication. It is a formidable prospect.

Let us say at once that there does exist a panacea for all this suffering. Go, O Amateur Gentleman, as we have already counselled you to choose your clothes and to confront the master of hirelings, in a spirit of humility. Remember the ostrich, who conceals her head in the sand, and keep well in the middle of the largest flock that you can find. Reflect that there is safety in numbers.

Obvious Danger of Being Wrong Way Up

You are certain, O Amateur Gentleman, to neglect this advice. We have already suspected that you are a subaltern. You are dreaming, at this very moment, of a series of events in which you, nasconded through unnatural foresight on the right side of the covert, get away alone with the master, huntsman, hounds and fox. After a point of twenty-five miles you are going to be left alone with hounds, are going to roll him over in the open, and, after performing all the last rites yourself, you will trot home thirty miles to kennels, arriving late at night with all the hounds about you and the bloody mask at your saddle bow.

We think it more proper not to ask you where your saddle bow is, or how you intend to fix the mask there; not to inquire how you propose to keep the hounds about you on the way home, or how you will get on with them during the last rites. We once knew an individual who did experience this extraordinary series of events, and it has left him a broken man. He arrived, excessively anxious to rescue the mask, but dared not trust his life to the howling mob. After several definite growls and one or two good-natured bites, he stood vaguely beside the mêlée, crying out "Tally ho!" occasionally—he was uncertain of the correct form of address—in a weak and querulous voice. Then the dogs sat down for a time and scratched themselves for fleas, drank water out of a ditch, smelt him in rather a menacing way, and dispersed in all directions. He lost his way home.

The Amateur Gentleman will be entertaining these ambitions, whatever advice we may give him, so the best possible advice will be that which can be most consistent with such a state of mind. Curiously enough it is possible to give good advice, even for such disordered thinkers.

We take it, O Amateur Gentleman, that you are contemptuous of all your three hundred and eighty-seven fellow sufferers, and that you are anxious to join the ranks of those eight persons previously referred to, who may now be dubbed the First Flight. We choose to overlook the fact that, on your hireling from the livery and bait stables, it is perfectly impossible for you to do so. Let us close our eyes to the obvious and see what advice you can be given.

Forget about Pavlov's taboos. The colour of your coat is immaterial, so long as it keeps the water out, and the way you hold your crop is not important, so long as you are able to open gates. If you can contrive to rid your mind—it will need a definite and almost physical effort, like throwing furniture out of a window—of all taboos, emulations and gentilities, if you can, moreover, contrive to open it to all the balance and common sense of the real world (so different from the high world, as the French call it) then nothing in the hunting calendar can do you harm. Every single rule in hunting, or every rule that is worth a farthing, is a matter of common sense. You come to a field with a lot of little emerald blades sprouting in it, and you recognise, if you are a normal and happy human being, that some farmer has planted autumn wheat or oats. He does not want to see your clumsy hoof-marks, and those of all those other hundreds, plunging across the labour of many weeks. You go round. You see the spread of hounds surging towards the position of your restive horse, and you know that he will kick at them if they come too close. You turn his head towards them, so that he cannot kick. You are following the hounds as they begin to work out a line, and the master is following them also, with an expression of torment on his face. The field is pressing upon them, dangerous to them, urging them beyond their mark. You keep behind the master, to give the hounds a chance. It is they who must catch the fox. The field is beginning to canter, to gallop: things are beginning to move. But the *master and huntsman* are in control of the hounds, so you sensibly keep behind.

Strive, then, to see as much of the hunt as possible: be contemptuous, if you must be, of all the other hag-ridden sheep who follow as best they may the instincts of the herd; but keep an alert eye and a modest soul. Ride hard, but use your *common sense*, and God will save you from the insults of the master and the imprecations of his bilious secretary.

That Man's Horse Kicks

§ 7

AN AVERAGE DAY

WE feel that the Amateur Gentleman, if he is faced
with his first hunt, may be thankful for a description
of an average day. His hireling has been ridden on by
a groom, together with several others, and he himself
has driven over to the Cock and Pye, where Monday's
meet is advertised for eleven o'clock. It has been difficult at first to find his way to this rural outpost, but
now he is beginning to meet enormous horse-boxes
drawn into the side of the road and anxious-looking
gentlemen trotting along in red coats, trying to get
their reins sorted out, and reserved, dark-coated,
bowler-hatted second horsemen, with hunting crops
tied round their backs. He is obviously on the right
road, and this must be the right village, and there,
yes, is the groom he remembers seeing at the stables
—though he is somewhat confused to discover that he
cannot recognise the horse which had been selected for

51

him. The groom chooses the horse out of the bunch which he is holding—it looks much smaller and darker than it did in the stables—and settles the stirrups for him—but surely one feels longer than the other?—and tightens the girths. The gentleman has, of course, arrived too early, and when these operations have been concluded he has leisure to look about him. The hounds have just trotted up from a side road, and are sitting on a grass patch in front of the public house, looking bored and important. The huntsman, with a look of resolution and self-defence, is seated upon his horse in the middle of them, engaged in taking off his hat to generous tips. Those who gave him five pounds last Christmas get a cap right down to the horse's shoulder, one pound comes down to the poll, while others are received with ill-veiled contempt. The master, with a haunted look on his face, is going round effusively shaking hands with farmers, as if he were playing Postman's Knock. He is afraid that he is going to miss one of them, or forget his name, with the result that some more wire will go up or the hunt be forbidden to ride over certain fields. The nobility and gentry are being driven up in a ceaseless stream of low-hung motor-cars, in which they crouch in defiant positions, desperately trying to keep their top hats from getting rumpled. The lower classes are hanging about the village street and the cottage doors, eyeing their superiors with open mouths which display their frank amazement that such people can exist. Their superiors, such of them as have already arrived, feel the same amazement that the lower classes can exist, but display their better breeding by ignoring that existence.

Our gentleman has ill-advisedly got upon his horse a good ten minutes before the hounds are likely to move off and is now a general target of interest from both parties. The village children point him out to one another with cries of genuine admiration, while the Misses Fotheringay, who are doing up their horses' girths on either side of him, talk through him with perfect insouciance about darling Diana's divorce, as if he were a telephone. A few late-coming military gentlemen with dubious horses are visible on the outskirts of the village, prancing about and kicking one another with a hollow noise. The middle-aged followers, or those bachelors whose nerve has completely broken, are coming out of the Cock and Pye with glazed expressions, wiping their moustaches and calling out broken pleasantries to one another in order to keep their courage to the sticking point. A few athletic young ladies in tweeds, and even a gentleman in shorts wheeling a bicycle, are standing by in a very knowing way and occasionally exchanging important remarks with the huntsman. These people are conscious that everybody else is conscious (but they are not) that though their families may have come down in the world they themselves are able to tell a crop from a whip. Being unable to afford the larger subscriptions, they subscribe to *Horse and Hound*, and carry on endless debates in the letter columns of that paper about the nomenclature of the crop and kindred subjects. At last a very dirty and disgraced old gentleman, dressed as a scarecrow and covered in mud, is led up to the huntsman for a few confidential whispers, and now the hounds are ready to move off. Nobody has spoken to us for ten minutes, and we have had the good sense to speak to nobody.

The hounds, huntsman, master and whips are in front of the cavalcade; then follow a score or so of red coats discussing (*a*) Diana's divorce; (*b*) the scan-

dals of the Hunt Ball; (c) Who Got Drunk Last. We
station ourselves about half-way down the procession,
which is at present in a very ragged state, nothing like
the compact and tedious serpent which it will be our
pleasure to sample later. It stretches out behind us,
through grooms, second-horsemen, perspiring late-
comers, chauffeurs, and doctors hurrying to vital
maternity cases but unable to get by. The draw at
Nelson's Bushes is over a mile away.

Nelson's Bushes proves to be a low, small, scrubby
woodland of about fifty acres, whose trees were cut
down in the Great War. The business end of the hunt
quickly vanishes inside it, and the field splits into two
groups, the late-comers still arriving. These groups
consist of those who believe that the fox will go away
on the far left of the wood, and those who believe he
will go away on the far right. Each group is thronged
about a gate. We select one of the two groups—it
makes no difference which—and stand wedged against
a lady who turns round and says accusingly, "My
horse kicks." Not being sharp enough to say the same
thing to the people who are pushing behind us, we
retain our position and wait for the kick. After a bit
the same lady, but this time without turning round,
remarks in a loud voice: "Some people are not
gentlemen."

A diversion is now caused by the hindermost man
of the left-hand (our) group, who decides that he had
rather be the hindermost man of the right-hand
group at the other side of the field. He canters off,
followed by the whole of the left-hand group, under
the mistaken idea that the fox has gone away on the
other side. He is now the middle man of the combined
groups, and the lady with the kicking horse is behind
us, so that both of us feel pleased with ourselves: until

the new hindermost man turns the tables by starting a stampede in the opposite direction. Nobody has heard the horn or seen anything of the hounds for some time. Every time we find ourselves behind the lady with the kicking horse she turns round and scowls at us, while every time we find ourselves in front of her, her horse begins to munch our horse's tail. She then says warningly to her neighbours: "I believe that man's horse kicks," until she has finally succeeded in isolating us by about ten yards from all human contact, and all are glaring at us with unconcealed hatred.

In the middle of these manœuvres a faint tooting noise is heard and a more definite panic than usual sets in towards one of the gates. The scowling lady passes us at top speed and charges the struggling mob who are now blocked at the gate. Her impetus carries her through about a dozen places ahead of us, and we ourselves, after a prolonged wait and knocking our knee on the gatepost, emerge into a new field. It is full of the same stream of people, now thinned out by the jam, all galloping for the next gate in view. We bow our head as the showers of mud begin to fly in our face, and by the time we have raised it again we are out into the third field. Here our heart begins to tighten, for there is no gate and the procession has moved into line abreast. A small crowd of disconsolate persons seems to be trying to shove its way through the hedge at the corner of the wood, like an ostrich concealing its head in the sand, but others are noticeably leaping. We can see five or six broad-shouldered backs which are going at the fence in different places. These are the remnants of the first flight. (Our actual place in the race at present, if you want to know, is 137th.) They are over and gone while we are still approaching, some over high places and some over low ones, and fortunately four of them have made holes. The holes are quickly adopted by those in front of us, and, by the time we get there, there are four queues waiting to jump at the four gaps. All the members of these queues are cursing each other feverishly, some exclaiming: "Damn you, can't you give me room to jump?" Others: "Damn you, don't jump in front of me." Others: "Damn you, don't jump behind me." And others more simply: "Damn you."

It is our turn now, much more quickly than it was at the gate, and here we go over the few remaining twigs, not very gracefully but safely, amid a shower of damns. Let us feel for our stirrups quickly and continue the chase, towards that little well-laid hedge which is impervious to blows. The first flight have made no impression upon it, and the queue-population is having to choose its own places. Their backs are bobbing up and down, and here we come ourselves— Lord, what strong branches they look for tripping up a horse!—and, look, we are safely over. What a pace, we do declare.

The hounds must be quite a mile in front by now, for we have seen nothing of them since the huntsman led them into covert, but here is a gate which will bring us in their direction. The pace and the two leaps have halved the field already, so that there will be no waiting at the gate. We have merely to charge through it after the man in front.

The third fence is a straggly sort of creature with some timber in last year's gaps, too high to leap except at the timber, and without a gate. See, here is the scowling lady in front of us, cantering at the timber for all she is worth, and see (what a joke!) her horse has refused the obstacle and is carrying her off in a nervous circle towards the right. Hark how she blasphemes. It is our turn now, and our horse does exactly the same; while the lady, in high hysteria, curses us for jumping in front of her.

While we are following her round in circles and getting upbraided for jumping out of turn—but unfortunately our horse won't jump—a very stout and perspiring gentleman comes sailing up from the rear, out of all control, and his horse runs straight through the rails without apparent discomfort, thus reducing the gap to its original state of safety last year. The scowling lady pays no further attention to us, but scrambles through in his wake, just before the inevitable queue has formed. We are too slow to get a good place in this and have to waste several valuable seconds waiting for a go. The go brings us mysteriously into a lane by a gate; and there everybody is, steaming and scowling and panting, exactly where we started from five minutes ago.

Admittedly the burst may take a slightly longer time, and we may even get as many as a dozen fences, but it seems kinder to spare the reader the tedium of a repetitive report. The run already invented may be taken as a typical one, containing most of the incidents which are likely to take place in a greater length of time, and now there is nothing to be done except to resume the original series of panics from gate to gate. The huntsman is back in Nelson's Bushes, and for the next half-hour it will be our fate to emulate the shuttlecock outside.

Something has gone wrong. Either the fox has hidden somewhere, or else there never was a fox. We have no means to determine which of these is the correct solution, for we have never been in a position to view the hounds, far less their quarry. But the fact remains that the master has decided to give up Nelson's Bushes and to move on to Wellington Copse.

It is now that we shall begin to form a true estimate of our hireling's peculiarities. The hounds have come out of covert and the procession has fallen in behind them *en route* for the next draw, which is two miles away. This one is a compact procession, a genuine squadron in column of four abreast. Its pace varies, not with the pace of the leading horseman (who might succeed in setting a steady trot), but with that of the leading hound. The average velocities of hound and horse are in no sphere of their activities sympathetic. We sit upon our hireling, who is razor-backed and has a violent trotting action, nervously following a military gentleman whose horse has a red ribbon on its tail. This means that if we go too close we may be kicked. Every time that Rattler turns round at the head of the procession to bite the base of his spine or to inspect some passing aroma, the hunt officials, trotting along with plenty of space before and behind them, moderate their speed in order to evade doing him a mischief; the master, who is at the head of the cavalry and still has a good deal of elbow-room, then draws rein in sympathy. The rank behind the master is on its best behaviour, and pauses without bumping him.

We have heard the clash of wagon after wagon as the goods train draws to rest, but the present experience is not quite the same. For one thing, none of the horses, except perhaps ours, is actually made of metal, and so they do not clash. Some of them are very expensive horses with amenable mouths and vigilant riders who are able to stop them at a touch, without collision. Others of them are intelligent enough to turn slightly to one side or the other, thus running up between the horses in front, instead of running into them. Not so, unfortunately, the hireling which has fallen to our lot.

Twenty-five years of age, and long resigned to the inequalities of fate, our horse shows by the deep pits over his eyebrows that he has reached the heaven of philosophy. He is a stoic philosopher, probably. In his mouth (this definitely is made of metal) they have placed a snaffle bridle so that we can hurt him as little as possible. He likes it. It is a kind of sling to support his head in. By totally relaxing the muscles of his neck he can leave it to us to support the front end, even if he is forced to carry us on the back. Resigned, experienced, negligent, semi-supported, deep in thought about Free Will and Predestination, the horse advances at a dogged pace.

There are two palliations for the ache in our arms: either we can cross the reins and hold them tight against his withers (which makes the withers support the head) or we can slowly pull his head from side to side, in order to prevent him from falling quite asleep. Neither of these courses will stop him from ramming the red ribbon at every diminution of pace, and the latter course may not appeal to us, on the grounds of appearance. As the horse has already attracted a good deal of attention by forging continuously—that is, by clashing his feet together as he walks—and by tripping absent-mindedly over every inequality of surface, we may prefer not to draw further attention upon ourselves by giving him the appearance of a sufferer from the blind staggers. Whatever we do, we shall have reason to bless the " hound jog," in which, for two miles, we shall have suffered from cramp in the arms, curses from in front, and the imminent possibility of being mangled with a kick.

Wellington Gorse is an interminable woodland or tangle, also de-forested in the late war. Into its rides, which stretch for miles in every direction, the whole regiment is allowed to proceed: and, what is more, is allowed to remain in peace for the next forty-five minutes. There is little to do during this period of time, except periodically to make our horse face in the opposite direction, and continuously to play the part of an inanimate telephone while the better acquainted members of the field, profoundly thankful for this brief armistice, continue their conversation about Diana. Occasionally the master or the huntsman, each with a few hounds, will go madly galloping across a distant ride, each pursuing a different fox, or our whole main body may thunder off to a different locality which seems more suitable for the discussion of divorce.

It will be in the course of one of these changes of milieu that we find ourselves outside the Gorse, and the morning's run being repeated. The runs will differ in no respects, unless we happen to fall off or to come across water; and it will be considered perfectly respectable to go home at *half-past two*, provided that we are not equipped with a second horse. It will be considered cowardly to go away before.

A word may be written in conclusion, upon the subject of falling off. It is important to remember that when you fall off you have not had a fall. A fall, which is a collapse accompanied by the collapse of the animal, is respectable and even noble: a falling off is done without the prostration of the animal and is considered a disgrace. There is, as the Amateur Gentleman may have noticed, a great deal of disgrace in hunting, a great deal of disgrace and recrimination and a great many damns. The gentleman will notice that as the people fall off they say, "Damn," just as they said it to each other on the other side of the fence, when they were only preparing to make the tumble. On riding home in the evening and thinking over the experiences of his first hunt, he may wonder why he has laid out five or six guineas in order to be damned all day. The reason why he was damned is simple, and would have been explained to him in a few words by Pavlov. People only swear, as dogs bark, because they are afraid.

Respectable, Even Noble

PART II

SALMON FISHING

Pensée in February

§ I

TYPES OF SALMON RIVER

THERE are four main types of salmon river in these islands: *The Financier's*, or water of which half a dozen inferior pools were withdrawn at £50,000 at the last sale but two—the sales are pretty frequent because the financiers keep getting put in prison; *The Laird's of That Ilk*, or water of unknown value because it has never passed out of the possession of The Ilk, and probably never been fished by them; *The Hotel*, or water of known inferiority which is fruitlessly flogged by such members of the rising bourgeoisie who cannot get their noses in anywhere else; and *Worm Water*, which is patronised by a solitary solicitor of great age who caught a salmon there in 1881 while fishing for trout and has since been back every year (the fishing is free) with a bouquet of worms threaded on enormous hooks. All these waters can be defined within a single *pensée* which occurred to us while fishing a heavy spate, in a snowstorm, in February, before the fish had run up: "If you are a millionaire, you can afford to own a catch which is full of salmon, in which case, why trouble to catch them?   If you are not a millionaire, you cannot afford to own a catch which has any salmon in it at all, in which case why trouble to catch them?"

The Financier's water is situated in El Dorado, and any one financier may during a good season kill five hundred fish of which those below 20 pounds are

Rowed by Indignant Scotsmen

called small and those above 30, large. As his rental will be in the neighbourhood of £2,500 per annum, these fish will have cost him £5 apiece, a figure which is considerably above their market value, but not so much so as is the case with the pheasant, which will be dealt with in a later section. Uneconomic as is the prospect, exclusive of rates, it is found that financiers are not deterred by it. They have been so economic all their lives that now, sitting back to enjoy the fruits of their various bankruptcies after fifty years, they are only too glad of a little change. They are rowed about the water in brightly painted boats by indignant Scotsmen (to whom they are very rude, as is fitting with servants), and as they dabble their gaily-feathered hooks in the murmuring water, so do the flotillas of enormous fish fight it out among themselves which shall have the first bite.

The Laird of the Ilk owns water on one of the smaller though excellent Scottish streams, say the Deveron or the Awe. But he is ninety-seven years of age and lives at Monte Carlo, having since the early years of last century been quite sick of the Ilk and interested in practically nothing but steam trams. His water is fished (*a*) by a friend of a nephew of his great-grandson, to whom he occasionally gives a grudging permission for the snow-water in February; (*b*) by a ghillie who goes down once a week with a hand line and kills three fish in ten minutes for the Laird's table; (*c*) by a certain Major Green, who, since 1903, has been under the misapprehension that this water belongs to him, owing to a conversation which he then had with the McInvert of McInvert's keeper. The McInvert, who also lives in Monte Carlo and collects sea shells, has let a totally different stretch of water to the Major. This water is situated upon the other coast of Scotland, and is fished by the editor of *Rivers in Britain*, who discovered it accidentally during one of his tours in 1908, and has since had the sense to keep it dark. Major Green, the ghillie, and the friend of the nephew of the great-grandson often clash over their fishing rights, but as they all feel that there is something wrong somewhere, they prefer to leave it at that.

Hotel Water is perfectly uneconomic for all concerned, except the landlord who lets it. The stretches on either side of it hold some good pools which either command a high rental or are reserved because of their goodness for the landlord's own recreation. The

Hotel Water, which lies between these stretches, has been cursed with some sort of blight and recognised for the last fifty years as hopeless. It is therefore let to an hotelkeeper, at a rental which is exaggerated by the high prices on either side, on the grounds that it can be of no use to any one else. The hotelkeeper, in his turn, vainly attempts to win back his outlay by charging half a dozen retired business men 5 guineas a week each, plus 8/6 a day ghillie, plus 15/- a day salmon fishing, plus £1 a fish. The latter fee is rarely earned, but the hotelier just manages to keep his head above water by catering for the summer tourists who are making in their thousands for the Pass of Glencoe, and they do not care a fig about fishing, anyway.

Worm Water is a subject which we would commend to the attention of the Amateur Gentleman. It is a matter for melancholy reflection that less than a hundred years ago all salmon fishing was virtually free, while in earlier times the self-respecting retainers of noble northern families would stipulate in their contracts of service that they were not to be given salmon for dinner more than twice a week. But that self-satisfied and cruel old humbug Isaac Walton, with his crucifixion of frogs and his eternal condescension from Piscator to Venator, somehow succeeded in fixing the attention of the upper classes upon fish— presumably as a means of humiliating each other far more brutally and improbably than Holmes ever humiliated Watson, if the *Complete Angler* is anything to go by—and free water gradually began to go out of circulation. A few moments' conversation with any ghillie past middle-age will show us that even within his own memory the rent of a given piece of water has risen by thousands per centum. This rise has taken place in all waters where the salmon has been found to be susceptible of temptation with the sunken fly— the method of temptation still the most common and, until 1903, the one invariably pursued. Since 1903, however, a new means of duping the Salmonidæ has been discovered: the method of greased-line fishing with a lightly-dressed fly which, although valuable at all seasons of the year provided that the air is warmer than the water, is particularly suitable for low summer water. It was the low summer water which had been regarded, until 1903, as totally unsuitable for the accepted practice of the sunken fly and which, under the scornful reputation of being possible only with the worm, has therefore remained at a low rental and sometimes even at none at all. Here the solicitor of 1881 caught a salmon when trout fishing with the dry fly (i.e. when using the greased line method by mistake, before Mr. Hills had time to invent it), and here he has since frequented with his worming tackle, catching two or three free salmon every year because the stretch has possessed the reputation of being impossible among orthodox anglers. His main terror during all these years has, of course, been that some interfering young gentleman should come along and kill a salmon on the fly; thus giving the place a correct fishing reputation, causing the impoverished little hotel which owns it to make a charge for the fishing, and quite spoiling his happy preserve by throwing it into the thousand-per-centum market of orthodox rivers. The hotel is on the upper reaches of the river, holds no fish in the spring, and possesses at present only the solicitor's summer season.

We make these revelations only because we are particularly fond of the reader, but we do suggest that an observant Amateur Gentleman who can master the greased line can still with luck congratulate himself upon not having been born too late to get his hook into a salmon at reasonable cost. He has been born too late to catch the sunk fly bus, but still not quite too late for the greased line in Worm Water. We have ourselves ousted the solicitor (who committed suicide), but we do not feel that we know the reader quite well enough to tell him the exact locality of this particular grave.

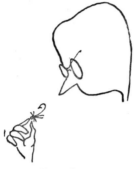

Intellectual Persons

§ 2

REASONS FOR FISHING

FISHING is exclusively the recreation of intellectual persons and of lunatics, but lunatics who are mad through an excess of mental development rather than the reverse. The reason is again a psychological one. The Amateur Gentleman will be aware that he is divided into layers, the top bit, called the Conscious Mind, being a great deal smaller than the bottom bit, which is called the Unconscious. Almost all psychologists will be ready to tell him that he is like an iceberg, of which we understand that only one-eighth part appears above the surface. The rest, the Unconscious, is in the water.

Water is always closely connected with the Unconscious, and of course there are fish in water. When, therefore, the Amateur Gentleman is particularly intellectual or conscious (*c.f.* " *Hallo, Unconscious,*" as a greeting between persons of low mental development), he will enjoy to sit on the top of his iceberg and to pull out the fish. Each fish which he hoists out of the Unconscious and consumes is something added to his conscious intellectual powers, and this is why the Prime Minister and other noble and intellectual persons were always getting photographed in waders just before the budget speech. The old idea that fishing could be defined as a stick with a worm on one end of it and a fool on the other is completely fallacious: for the allocation is far more likely to turn out to be Einstein waving a bunch of feathers.

Individuality in Hats

§3

CORRECT COSTUME

THE right dress for fishing is more elastic than that prescribed for hunting, so much more so that many authorities have preferred to describe it by its negative rather than by its positive qualities. It would be wrong, for instance, or at any rate exceptional, to go fishing in full hunting dress. You would be liable to stick your hook into the back of your top hat when casting. In the same way, it is incorrect to wear a fireman's helmet—which would attract lightning.[1] Full dress uniform of a martial nature is inadvisable, owing to the flash of cuirasse, epaulettes, etc., which would distract the fish, and ballet skirts (for women) are considered unwise for reasons similar to those adduced in describing the belting of waders—see p. 70.

[1]We feel it is high time that a courageous and experienced sporting scientist should devote his talents to an exhaustive dissertation on electric storms. It is a melancholy fact that hunting, being carried on in the winter months, is almost the only gentlemanly occupation (tobogganing can scarcely be called

73

Apart from these minor prohibitions, which are, after all, only the result of common sense, almost any costume can be worn by the fisherman so long as it will stand up to bad weather. Some early-season anglers go so far as to wear oilskins and sou'wester, although we ourselves are inclined to recommend a fuzzy tweed suit for all but the foulest gales. The waistcoat, and indeed the coat, can be left on the bank in hot weather, while, if it comes on to rain, the wiry protruding tendrils of tweed will hold the raindrops away from the main cloth, making a dewy cloak which is beautifully waterproof.

Most fishers prefer to express their individuality in

so) which does not expose its devotee to the danger of being struck by lightning; and that in hunting there is the other danger of tumbling off the horse. Even in golf, although this is not a gentlemanly sport, thousands of suburban stockbrokers are annually and some think rightly blasted, together with their caddies, as they cluster with iron implements round the pins, trees and tee-boxes of their melancholy pursuit. Terrified as all sensible people are by thunderstorms, none of us dares to admit it, and the position remains a vicious circle in which the simple sportsman is carried by his own death-dealing implements to certain death. In September, the worst season for such disturbances, the petrified marksman plods across vast uplands, the highest point for miles around, holding his steel fowling-piece as much as possible by the wood and conscious that his stomach is surrounded by a belt of live percussion cartridges. High on the moorland sources of the river, and knowing that water is an excellent conductor for electricity, the trembling angler waves his fishing rod, like Faraday trying to attract the lightning.

There is only one certain sanctuary, and that is to lie down flat on the face, as far as possible from rod, gun, cartridge, tree, or anything else. This course is seldom open to the sportsman, for he usually pursues his sport in company, and where two or more persons are gathered together, death is invariably preferable to dishonour.

In order to meet this need, and beating the 420th page of Messrs. Hardy's catalogue by a short head, we have perfected and patented a portable lightning conductor which can be strapped to sportsmen before setting out. It can be worn for shooting, but is primarily designed for the angler, being 25 feet in height—or longer than any fishing rod now in use. Clamped round the neck and waist, it is scarcely noticeable among the other impedimenta (rod, wading staff, gaff-net, priest, magnifying glass, collapsible stool, haversack, cast damper, cast box, fly boxes, bait boxes, spare reel, spare rod, line drier, luncheon basket, set of tools, gauges, balances, disgorger, tackle releases, etc.) which Messrs. Hardy have proved necessary to be carried by every thinking sportsman. Our own patent is, indeed, collapsible, and can be used in times of fair weather as rod, wading staff, gaff-net, priest, magnifying glass, etc. All the instruments mentioned above have been ingeniously fitted to it by our own staff of engineers, and when used for shooting a kite can be flown from the top. This keeps down the birds. Price £500.

their hats. The general uniform of a tweedy nature —anything which would not look outré on a scarecrow—is accepted by all, but in the hat a certain virtue still resides. The reason for this may lie in the intellectual nature of these persons, which has already been discussed, that might tend to make them value their heads. Some ornament them with sou'westers, some with deer-stalkers or Twa-Snooted-Bonnets, some with a kind of elastic solar topee made of tweed, some merely with the oldest hat of any kind which they can steal from a bird-scarer and adorn with their own flies. Short of the busby and the black cap worn by judges at murder trials, almost every form of headgear constructed by man has been attempted at one time or another by the angling fraternity, and it should be the Amateur Gentleman's earnest endeavour to provide himself with a headgear of real distinction. There is one proviso, however. Every genuine angler wears his hat for a *reason*. It is no good wearing a bowler hat simply because it is a bowler: you must wear it because it makes an excellent line-drier or cast-damper or receptacle for live bait. If you decide to wear an airman's helmet, you must do so because it prevents the mosquitoes from biting your neck, forehead and ears (as a matter of fact this is an excellent plan, and has saved many lives in Lapland, where the mosquitoes are as big as grouse), while, if you select to patronise a jockey-cap, you must do so because it keeps the rain out of your neck when put on back to front. Every good fisherman wears his cap with a difference, and preferably in order to have a difference with you about his cap.

There is little more to be said about the clothing of the angler, except that reason seems to dictate that all colours—whether of haberdashery or of tailoring

—should be subdued, and that all coats—not only the light (unlined) mackintosh—should be capable of being buttoned firmly round the neck. If we except mittens, which can be used for shooting also, footwear is the only subject that remains.

Although authors of humble birth and straightened circumstances, or we would not be writing this book for the amateur gentleman who probably finds himself in like condition, we do have to affirm that expense is either absolutely essential or absolutely inessential in the matter of the feet while fishing. There are two ways about it, neither more nor less. If the honoured reader is a man of invincible constitution, he may fish with no special provision for his legs at all, wading into February water just as he would walk into a drawing-room, with or without removing his trousers. (Sooner or later every salmon fisherman is bound to wade, though not to walk into a drawing-room without his trousers.) If he is not of invincible constitution, and does not enjoy to stand soaked to the armpits in a snowstorm waiting to get dry, then we are sorry to say that no other course is open to him except to buy himself full waders, socks and brogues. Nothing made of rubber, and we risk a large number of libel actions in saying so, is of any use at all. We have spent more than half our fortune on Wellingtons and goloshes and thigh-boots, in the attempt to do without waders—spent enough money to equip half the Board of Agriculture and Fisheries with the very best waders—and never with the remotest success.

There are two things wrong with all substitutes. First, no really British angler can avoid going in too deep for the abbreviated article. (It is easy to avoid going too deep for full waders, because, by the time you have got up to your waist in any real river, you are so frightened by the current and hampered in casting with high elbows that you are only too glad to come out again at once.) Second, wet rubber—whatever its other properties—is not adhesive. Standing on a smooth submerged rock in even the most deeply corrugated rubber soles is not perilous. It is impossible.

If the Amateur Gentleman is obstinate, or has perhaps already bought himself something with rubber soles, he will shortly find himself at the shoemaker's, clamouring for nails. The shoemaker will reply (which is true) that nails don't stay in rubber. They come out again at once. Let the gentleman now insist upon steel *screws*, and these will keep him upright for about twenty-four hours, before they too wear out and cast his bread upon the waters.

There is one piece of etiquette about fishing costume which deserves to be obeyed, and this is the rule that full waders should never be tied or belted at the top. The reason for this is that, if you should happen to lose your feet, the air confined at the top of your waders will rush to your toes, thus causing you to proceed downstream with your legs in the air and your head under water, a position which is considered indecorous.

Considered Indecent

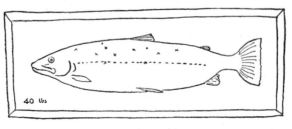

An El Dorado

§ 4

IT should be explained before any detailed discussion of this topic that there are two kinds of fishermen. We have met them both, fishing the Laird of That Ilk's water in Scotland. Major Greene is provided with the following outfit: one or more cottages, containing one or more ghillies; one gun-room, containing rod cabinet; some boats; one long rod box outside the gun-room, in which the rods can be temporarily stored without taking them down; one 17-foot Norwegian salmon rod, with reel and line to match; one 15-foot Hi Regan, with ditto; one 12½ foot Wye, with ditto; one 10-foot Murdoch spinning rod, with spinning reel and line to match; four assorted rods of unknown origin; one fly cabinet containing twenty dozen flies at about 3/- each; one mortuary containing bottled prawns, sandeels, gudgeon, dace, roach and sprats, besides a drawer or two of artificial phantoms, Devons, swallow-tails, spoons and orenos;

78

one wardrobe containing waders, brogues, water-
proofs, hats; one large suitcase or haversack full of
gut casts, traces and various appliances for wetting,
drying, oiling or transporting the same; several gaffs
and wading staffs; some knee pads; some aluminium
weights for practice casting; an angler's knife (unused)
containing among other delights a pair of scissors,
disgorger, file, lance, stiletto, tweezers and screw
driver; two tackle releases; a zip-fastening Bait
Carrier and Protector Pouch; some sponge rubber
cushions for boat seats; some rod rests for trolling;
a combined folding stool and tackle case; half a dozen
thermometers; a water telescope; and an angler's
pipe whose fire consumes the nicotine.

The other kind of angler is the ghillie who goes
down periodically to kill a fish for the Laird's table.
This gentleman possesses: one composite rod 20 feet in
length, partly greenheart, partly split cane and partly
plain oak; one reel with enormous line roughened
like a file; one cast discarded in 1927 by Major Greene;
one hook with three strands of pheasant tail still
adhering to it. He also has a snuff-box made out of
an old 1 oz. tin of shag tobacco.

The ghillie always kills seven times as many fish
as Major Greene, but it would be unwise to make
any invidious comparisons on that account. His
pre-eminence is not entirely due to his skill and only
partly due to his better tackle: the real reason being
that he has so much more time for fishing, as apart
from assembling his gear. But whatever the reason,
we desire to warn the Amateur Gentleman that he
will be wise if he does not laugh at Major Greene nor
exalt the ghillie above him. The ghillie would make
exactly the same purchases as the Major, if only he had
the money—*and so will the Amateur Gentleman.*

Fishing is, indeed, a mystery, a revelation, an El Dorado; but it has little or nothing to do with common sense. It is a visionary quest. The young fisherman may start, perhaps, with little better equipment than the ghillie's, and even with the determination to make do with the efficient minimum always; but he is bound to get hold of some money sooner or later—and what fisherman could spend his money on anything but tackle? Once inside that fatally exquisite shop in Pall Mall or Hereford or Belmont Street, Aberdeen, what fisherman can resist those glaring fishy eyes painted upon the Devon Minnow—eyes which, since the minnow revolves, will be perfectly invisible to the fish? Nobody can resist them. All fishing tackle is calculated to charm the angler rather than the angled, and for this reason it is difficult if not impossible to advise the Amateur Gentleman about his purchases. Young anglers have small stocks, old anglers large ones, simply because the longer you live as a questing angler the more time your fervid imagination will have in which to surround itself with beautiful and unnecessary equipment.

Confronted with this dilemma, we hit upon the plan of consulting a middle-aged angler, assuming that, having run about half the race, he would possess a sound average amount of tackle. He said:

"I am a man whose soul loves order, and I have reduced my travelling equipment to two packages, thus making it possible to carry *all* my fishing tackle in my own two hands. Without alteration of these two packages I am prepared to travel at any season of the year to any part of the British Isles and to fish at once.

"The first package contains the rods. One of them is a 17-foot fly rod, because, no matter what anybody may say, I believe that there are some rivers and winds which make a long cast or heavy line essential. The second is a 12-foot fly rod for the greased line, and it has a spare top by means of which it can be converted into a spinning rod. These are all the rods I have, and the package, which rolls up, would look like this if laid out flat upon the floor:

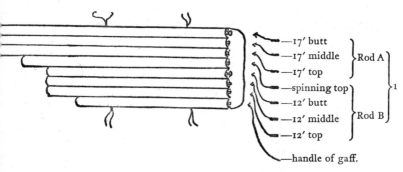

The whole is, in fact, a double rod cover made in one piece of strong waterproof twill, containing two rods and an extra top capable of converting one of them into a spinning rod. It also holds the handle of the gaff.

"The second package consists of a small fibre attaché-case which I purchased for two shillings at a stationer's. I constructed various compartments, boxes and fittings for its interior, out of stout cardboard, and sewed them in with twine. I then covered my seams inside and out with adhesive tape, to smooth my edges and to prevent water from passing through the holes made by the needle. I painted the whole a pleasing shade of Indian red and gave it four coats of varnish on top of the paint, inside and out, to make it thoroughly waterproof. When completed it looked something like a lady's dressing-case.

[1]Normal spare tops omitted for the sake of the diagram.

The two compartments marked A were designed to hold the two matched thermometers with which I could measure the air and water temperatures simultaneously. The compartment B contained artificial baits such as spoon, phantom, oreno, and Devon minnows, *both heavy and light*, and in several sizes, all with bits of cork upon the barbs. It also contained the traces, in fact most of the ironmongery. C was the ordinary japanned holder which would open in four

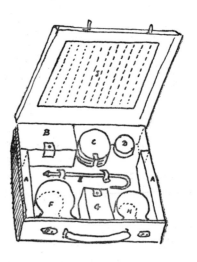

layers and contained gut casts from light to heavy. D was a tin of cerolene. (Both C and D were glued to the floor.) E was the gaff head. F and H were the compartments designed to hold my two reels, while the box G contained certain little necessaries such as the celluloid rings used for marking chicken's legs (useful in liberating snagged minnows) and a really stout piece of cord—for carrying home the prize. J was a square cork dinner mat with pipe-cleaners sewn over it in vertical lines. It was glued and stitched to the lid, and would carry, hooked into the pipe-cleaners, a good two hundred flies.

"You will now," continued the middle-aged angler, "be wondering how I make do with two reels when my rods are capable of being made up into three kinds—a 17-footer for the sunk fly, a 12-footer for the greased line, and a spinning rod. The compartment H contains the greased line reel for the 12-foot rod, with its greased line attached, and that is that. But F contains a wooden Nottingham reel with an ungreased heavy salmon line. Both reel and line are heavy enough to suit the 17-foot rod, when fishing the orthodox sunk fly. What about the spinning rod? Well, I dislike spinning, and only resort to it when there is no other possible alternative: and this does not happen very often. On the rare occasions when it does happen, I use the Nottingham reel with the check off, and find that even if the heavy line cannot be described as orthodox for spinning, yet it spins perfectly well with a little practice. I do not think this is hard on the line."

We immediately sat down with Messrs. Hardy's catalogue, and began to assess the price of all these articles if purchased at that store. Omitting the price of the flies, which this gentleman was in the habit of tying for himself,[1] and guessing the price of a 12-foot rod which would be convertible for spinning, we came to the conclusion that an Amateur Gentleman could set out to angle in any part of the British Isles, at any season of the year, for a preliminary outlay of about forty-three pounds inclusive. Inclusive, that is, of everything but salmon.

Such are the bare bones of the story,[2] and perhaps

[1] See Appendix A.

[2] The angler in question has since bought himself a line-drier, which he presumably carries slung round his neck.

it is best to leave it at that. At one extreme there stands the lawless urchin with a sixty-year-old fishing rod, bound in a hundred places, which has been given to him for nothing; his father, who is clever with his hands, has made him a wooden reel which works pretty well, and the line is little better than string; he has begged an old piece of gut from an angler who was here last year, and found an old fly in the heather. See, he is into a fish (which he will have to beach or tail); and God! how his young heart beats as he fights for it. Yet there, at the other pool, bless us if it isn't Captain the Hon. "Piggy" Plantaganet, and he is into a fish as well! See how motionless he stands, with what a noble indifference he pursues the battle. When they had got him up and dressed him this morning, and after they had given him a little food, his head ghillie decided to take him out with one of the latest spinning reels. Its mechanism was a little complicated, so the ghillie thought it best to do the actual casting for him, but once he was into a fish he handed it over to the captain. Notice the noble and gallant gentleman's statuesque calm. He just stands there and winds the handle. It is all he has got to do, actually: for this is one of those most modern and expensive organ-grinder's reels, which play the fish for you automatically so long as you will only go on turning. One ghillie stands at the captain's feet, holding a patent, collapsible, reversible, insoluble, non-inflammable gaff-cum-shooting-stick. One ghillie stands behind him, on either side burdened to the eyebrows with labour-saving devices: with rod-cum-line-drier, wading-staff-cum-telescope, fishing-cabinet-cum-tantalus, camp-bed-cum-salmon-net and with two small trunks containing lures and flies. See how the fish, maddened by the excitement, dashes up and down the stream, from bank to bank, wallows with a spanking noise, leaps with a thunderclap clean out of the water. See how Captain Plantaganet is a match for him, how Captain Plantaganet is winding on. But can it be true that Captain Plantaganet has gone to sleep?

Wrong Thing

§ 5

ETIQUETTE

THE upper classes are much more interested in doing the right thing than in doing the thing right. For this reason the Amateur Gentleman will lie awake many nights, turning over in his mind not whether he is going to enjoy fishing or kill many fish, or be a good fisherman, but whether he is going to make a fool of himself by violating some taboo of which this little book has stupidly left him in ignorance. We are anxious to relieve him of this fear, and have decided to devote a whole section to the right thing, in consequence.

Almost all the right things in fishing are related to the intimate life story of the fish. (By the way, among right people a "fish" is a salmon, while the other species are mentioned by their generic titles— trout, grayling, etc.) The Atlantic salmon begins as a pink egg, which, when fertilised by the milt of the cock fish, turns milky. These eggs are irresistible as bait, and the use of them is therefore illegal. It is also not a right thing, as are (*i.e.* wrong things) almost

86

all expeditious ways of killing the fish, such as: catching it in a net at the mouth of the river, spearing it by torchlight, frightening it ashore in a shallow pool, seducing it with worms, foul hooking it in summer water, shooting it, harpooning it, blowing it up with depth charges, hitting it with a hammer as it goes by.

The eggs hatch out into things whose photographs have to be seen to be believed, and these things in due course turn into small, dubious and flashing fish. We have an idea that such fish are called parr, but we are not set upon it. Anyway, they are only a few inches long and they dash about in the water for two years or so, occasionally assaulting the lures of the impatient fishermen. It is a wrong thing to kill the creatures. Upon perceiving a small fish doggedly holding on to the 6/o hook, which is nearly as big as itself, the Amateur Gentleman will reflect as follows: "I have been fishing for a week now, without catching anything, and here is a trout. It shall die." Now it quite likely is a trout; but, even if it is, it is not a big one. It may be a parr. The Amateur Gentleman should now ask himself whether the possible réclame consequent upon returning to the hotel with a three-inch trout is worth balancing against the hilarity and odium which will ensue should it turn out to be a baby salmon. When he has asked himself this question he should moisten his hand and release the small unfortunate without removing it from the water. He will catch it again, anyway, at the next cast.

Many angling writers take pains to describe the salmon parr to their pupils, in order to save them the mortification of doing the wrong thing. It will be seen that our method (that of putting back all fish under $\frac{3}{4}$ lb.) is more simple. After all, what is a fish worth under $\frac{3}{4}$ lb.? And, after all that, who could describe a salmon parr, anyway? It is a cross between a sardine and a perch.

When these creatures have lived the correct time in the river, as laid down for them in the Lonsdale Library, they go out to sea and eat cod. This is good for them, because cod are full of cod liver oil (or halibut liver oil, if in concentrated form) and they soon grow big, multiplying their weight by twenty or thirty times in the same period which gave them a few ounces' addition in fresh water.

They are now about four years old and feel that it is time they were having some little parr themselves. So they come back to the river they were born in, swim up it to the spawning redds, and fulfil their destiny as fish. The salmon fishing season occurs during this river journey, roughly from February to October (it varies with different rivers) and when the season is over the fish begin to spawn. After they have celebrated their nuptials they become completely depressed, disillusioned and cynical, hang about in the river until the winter is almost over, and then die of disgust, a perpetual warning against matrimony. They are now called Kelts.

The dying Kelt begins to drop down the river at the end of the close season, in a ravenous and exhausted state, and the early-season angler will hook several of them before the big spate has finally washed them all away.

Since ninety-nine out of every hundred Kelts are certain of a lingering death, often aggravated by indescribably horrible growths, anybody who was not a gentleman would think that the kindest thing to do with a Kelt would be to knock it on the head. On the contrary, an exaggerated courtesy is now extended to the repenting matron, possibly because anglers belong to the Capitalist classes whose interest it is to encourage the state of holy wedlock. It is the wrong thing to kill a Kelt, indeed almost the wrongest thing there is in fishing, like shooting foxes because the hunt can't keep them down.

To distinguish a Kelt from a fresh-run salmon is simplicity itself, once you have killed a few of the latter, but it is to be assumed that the Amateur Gentleman is not in such a position. If he had killed real salmon he would be a Professional Gentleman, and

Survival of the Fish

would have thrown this book away long ago in rightful disgust.

Unfortunately it is important to distinguish between Kelts and fresh-run fish while they are still in the water, because the act of removing the salmon from the water with a kind of steel meat hook plunged into its back is inimical to the prospects of any fish whose survival is of immediate interest to any of the parties concerned. Thus many authorities consider that the amateur would be well advised to refrain from gaffing any fish in the early spring, unless fishing in company with a ghillie who can look after that side of the question for him. On some rivers an enormous landing net is *de rigeur*.

The Kelt, after its saddening experience of the married state, fights with an envenomed hysteria more violent than that of the fresh fish, but the fight is also sooner out of it. When played to a standstill it may be examined in the water at the Gentleman's feet, and will be found to be a long, narrow, silver-pale fish with a haunted or wedded expression. Many infallible means of distinguishing between the two species are laid down by sporting writers, notably by comparing the colour of the gills, but as all these means assume (*a*) the presence or clear recollection of a real salmon for comparison, and (*b*) the Kelt's position on the bank for leisured examination, none of them can be of much assistance to the virgin angler with his fish in the water because he fears to gaff it out. It is therefore simpler to concentrate upon shape. The pallid Kelt's is the eel's belly and the pike's despair, the violet salmon's is the snow-white belly of the whale.

The Amateur Gentleman should not depress himself unduly by considering this problem. If he fishes with a ghillie, the ghillie will solve it for him; if he fishes alone, he has only to bury his mistakes. Once on the bank it is impossible to mistake a Kelt for a good fish and he need have no fear of taking the wrong kind home. Nor is any ethical principle involved. The fish will die in any case after he has played it out, so the use or otherwise of the final gaff becomes a question of artificial morals altogether. This fact should not, however, be mentioned in society.

Hurried Breakfast

§ 6

AN AVERAGE DAY

Iғ the Amateur Gentleman possesses a great deal of money he can immediately purchase a good salmon river, and two or three ghillies with their wives and dependants will naturally be included in the deal. In this case he will automatically become a Professional Gentleman (since the local master of hounds will need his subscription) and, the ghillies being perfectly able to hook, gaff, or indeed play his fish for him, he will no longer stand in need of the services offered by this invaluable little book. So our public must be assumed not to be in possession of a great deal of money.

The average day for such a public, which is probably too poor to belong to a good syndicate, even, must consist, if we leave out the deep and beautiful mystery of Worm Water, of one out of two alternatives : either the Amateur Gentleman must borrow a first-class river in February from some rich acquaintance who

knows there are no fish in it during that month, or he
must discover a good salmon fishing hotel. He should,
if a reasonably heavy drinker, be prepared to pay about
fifteen guineas a week at one of these resorts, inclusive
of fishing, ghillie, bed, board and drink. The hotel
will list its prices somewhat lower than his, but that
is what they are likely to average out at when the bill
comes round. It is at such an hotel that we shall be
most helpful in spending our average day. A description of the alternative average, on the rich February
river with no fish in it, would become monotonous.
It snows all the time in the latter case, and all you have
to do is to provide yourself with eleven empty bottles
of whisky and one full, together with a good supply
of celluloid chicken rings. The empty bottles are
attached one by one to the spinning line, by means of
the chicken rings, and floated off in the vain effort to
salvage snagged minnows. By the time you have
lost eleven traces and a few score yards of line, you
will have finished the contents of the twelfth bottle,
and it is then advisable to go home.

The average day on hotel water at its best time
(say May) begins at half-past eight, when the Amateur
Gentleman springs out of bed, full of optimism,
determination and constipation. He hurries downstairs, almost unshaven, and hastily gobbles (but does
not digest) a few mouthfuls of the excellent breakfast
served by this hotel. The hotel serves this breakfast
as a conscience offering, for it knows that no luncheon
except sandwiches is included in its five guineas a week.
In the course of the fevered meal the Amateur Gentleman calls confusedly between mouthfuls for tepid
water in a saucer (to soak his casts in), for his waders,
his line drier and various other oddments, which
occur to his maddened brain as being of cosmic im-

portance. He winds his line from the drier to the reel with one hand and feeds himself with alternate mouthfuls of porridge and gut cast with the other. All things having reached a kind of conclusion, and none having reached a complete one, he throws down his spoon and rushes out into the passage, under the stuffed salmon of 38 lbs., to pull on his waders. This done, he infuriates the lady of the house by bursting into the kitchen to claim his luncheon basket, not yet ready, and assembles all his gear in a pile on the front doorstep, so as to be ready for the car and the ghillies the moment they arrive. At this instant an elderly angler who is to share the car with him and to exchange beats in the afternoon comes slowly down the stairs to begin his breakfast.

The Amateur Gentleman may now sit down under the stuffed salmon for forty minutes or so, and he may pass his time in reflecting upon the following problems:

1. Do salmon take at any particular time of day?

2. If so, is this time (*a*) merely any time when you are not there, or (*b*) a particular time when you are not there?

3. For instance, do they perhaps take before breakfast and after dinner?

4. Would it be wise to warn the proprietor of this possibility and to arrange to fish from 6 a.m. to 11 p.m., or to sleep out on the bank?

The answer to all these questions is "No." The proprietor knows, and the aged angler now enjoying his breakfast knows, that not only do salmon not take before breakfast, but that they rarely if ever take at all. This is why the car and ghillies are not ready, for the proprietor supposes and the aged angler recognises as a fact that the famished fisherman will suffer more than the fed one in the almost certain event that neither of them sees a fish.

These matters having been satisfactorily pondered, the car and ghillies will arrive, and your doddering partner will come out of the breakfast-room wiping his moustache. Harrying everybody about in all directions, you will bundle the party into the motor, choose the nearer of the two beats, and arrange to be dropped at the nearest pool of this beat while the car goes on to drop your companion at the farthest pool of the farthest beat. By this means you hope to start fishing about twenty minutes before he does. You jump out of the car as it comes to a standstill, dig out your rod and tackle with trembling fingers, and practically run down to the river, urging a reluctant Highlander before you. It is at this moment, just as the car is disappearing up the glen, that you will remember your reel, which was left on the breakfast table. Sit down then, for the car will not be back for half an hour, and get the ghillie to tell you a few Highland legends. He probably knows none either.

If we were a truthful sporting writer we could end this description here, merely adding that from now onwards (as soon as the car has been back for the reel) you will continue to splash your line in the water and to disentangle your hook from trees, until it is time to go home. But we intend to give full value for money, and, since such things have been known to occur, you shall have a fish.

It is important to keep on good terms with the ghillie, and to remember that he has probably fished this water since before you were born. A good way of winning the affection and co-operation of a ghillie is to ask him to bring his rod and to fish down the water after you. Such a course of action will at the

same time deliver you from the great vice of ghillies
—supposed by many gentlemen to be a virtue—which
is, the habit of tying on your flies. By all means learn
knots from ghillies, and get them to show you how
to tie them, but do the actual job yourself. Then, if
anything does go wrong, you will know who is to
blame, and be spared much useless regret and indignation. The truest word ever spoken about this clumsy
world was: If you want to do anything well, do it
yourself. But in order to be allowed to do it yourself,
you will probably have to interest the ghillie in his
own fishing.

The ghillie leads you to the top of the pool, looks
dubiously at a rock, a rabbit hole and a tree stump,
and demands your fly-box. He opens this with
exaggerated precaution (who knows but what the
latest gadget perfected for these expensive southron
gentry may not contain a jack-in-the-box?) and peers
inside it with still greater dubiety. Finally he shuts
the box, which contains two dozen assorted lures at
three shillings each, and withdraws one of the two
rusty hooks, each adorned with half a moth-eaten
feather, which ornament his own hat. Do not attempt
to prevent him from making this first attachment,
but go down with it to the river-bank at the point
which he indicates, and begin to throw it sheepishly
in. If you are not an expert caster, do not pretend to
be one, nor produce any excuses, such as a new rod,
out of practice, veering wind, etc. Remember that
you are being watched by a past master in this lovely
art, and ask for advice if necessary.

You have fished half the pool now, paying particular attention, as the ghillie directed you, to that
smooth wet rock one-third of the way down. The
wind has been blowing diagonally upstream and only

one cast in three has truly reached its approximate destination, but apart from this, and apart from the feeling that you can't cast as far as you would like, and apart from the knot which has somehow tied itself in your gut cast and the bother which was caused when you got caught up in the ash tree, you feel that you have covered the water reasonably well, particularly that bit above the smooth rock. The gentle splash and subdued commotion which you now hear is the ghillie, who has hooked a fish behind you, just at that rock.

He is calling you now to come and run the fish. If your self-respect is of Homeric proportions, you will tell him that since he has hooked it he had better run it himself. If you are a humble man, you will accept his offer (which he will make easier for you by looking very cross at your preliminary hesitation) because even running a fish will give you a chance to learn something. He hands you the rod with only a gentle bend in it, holding it with one hand by the butt and putting no check on the reel except the mechanical one which is already there. You seize the rod, take hold of the handle of the reel, wind in a few turns and bend the rod double. "Too hard," says the ghillie. The fish shows for a moment near the surface, his great silver side looking rusty in the water, wallows another moment, and the fly, coming away, whistles past your ear to land on the bank behind you.

Amateur Gentleman, do not cry or curse. Reflect upon this misadventure with a mind that desires to better itself. The ghillie, who is an angler of the old school, said that you were too hard on the fish. But it was he who hooked it, and upon him rests the responsibility of the hold. For you can be too hard on a fish at the moment of hooking him, but you cannot be too hard afterwards—short of breaking your tackle. It stands to reason. A hold that is going to give will give. Ten minutes of fierce strain will not be any more likely to lose it than half an hour of light pressure: indeed, it will be less likely to lose it, just as you will be less likely to pull a nail out of a wall with one strong pull than with very many little wriggles. The fact that spring salmon have light mouths, a fact which will be advanced by the ghillie, has nothing to do with it. Once the hold is established, hard treatment is no more dangerous than light: it was the ghillie who established this hold, and you have no cause to reproach yourself.

But you will reproach yourself.

You will feel that you are a fool and a rogue to have missed the fish in the first place, letting the ghillie hook it behind you—more than 50 per cent of this was pure chance—that you are a scoundrel and an imbecile to have lost the glorious creature which he obtained. Barratry, simony, arson, matricide and every other tort, these you will consider to be your bedfellows, shame and remorse your only portion for the few remaining years of a disgraced and decrepit existence.

The next pool is Black Murdoch, a long broad elbow of water with the main current on the other side. There it has cut a small precipice out of the bank, while on your side the shingle slopes into the stream with a more gentle graduation down which it is necessary to wade. Black Murdoch means deep wading, and you look piteously at the ghillie because it seems quite impossible to fish it. The ghillie points sternly forward, indicating a position which will place a hawthorn tree exactly behind you, just within reach of your back-cast, while the elbow of Black Murdoch is exactly in front of you, just out of reach of your forward-cast. There is nothing for it but to wade in as far as possible without total immersion, pay out line, and do your best to reach the main current on the opposite side. If you ever had any ability to cast in the first place, it will vanish when you discover that a continuation of your previous action now means dipping your elbows and forearms into the water twice at each cast, while the force of the water against the submerged part of your body is such that any movement whatever is fraught with extreme peril. Go on, however, and splash about as best you may.

While you are sporting in the whirlpool, frozen between fury and tears in your inability to make more than one true cast out of six, the ghillie will sit down on the bank and go to sleep. He does this because after the briefest inspection he has realised that it will be politer not to watch you. If he did watch you, you would be paralysed by the suspicion that he was finding you amusing; but now that he does not watch you, you are infuriated by the suspicion that he finds you boring. You are just casting a malevolent glance at him over your shoulder, a glance in which indignation at being made to fish an apparently impossible distance, shame at being unable to fish that distance, and reproach for his seemingly callous indifference are striving for mastery, when you hear a splashing noise at the other side of Black Murdoch. Your last cast went astray and you are quite out of touch with your fly, which is, as far as you know, lying tangled in the slack at the edge of the current about fifty yards away. This is the reason why you have, as a matter of fact, hooked a beautiful fish which is making the splashing noise you noticed, and, since you are a beginner, it is almost certain to be a forty-pounder. You may now tighten up on your fish and retreat backwards out of the water, in the perfect certainty that the hold is good. You were not in contact with your fly and had no opportunity of striking. The current did all this for you, drawing the hook backwards into the corner of his jaw as he turned away, before you noticed anything, and he is firmly held. Come out as quickly as possible, hoping that the ghillie really was not looking after all.

It turns out that the fish is of at least thirty pounds, and you, after your experience of losing the last fish apparently through violent methods, will submit to every suggestion made by the ghillie. He for his part takes your hand right off the handle of the reel while the fish makes his first rush. He reiterates that if "He" wants to go you must let "Him" go, and that this will tire "Him" out. It does nothing of the sort, however, for this fresh and powerful fish merely takes advantage of the current, leaning against it on the other side just sufficiently to balance the timorous pull which has been dictated to you by your mentor. Two hours later, with arms feeling like those of that gentleman in the Bible who had to hold them up in the air while a battle was going on, you will be compelled, and the ghillie will inconsistently exhort you, to resort to the violent methods which you might as well have adopted in the first instance; and you will drag the fish into shallow water by main force. There the ghillie will pierce it with his meat hook, heave it ashore and bash it on the head. By that time you will have visited about three pools, walked several miles, seen your line five times down to the dangerous end of the backing, quarrelled twice with the ghillie and experienced all the limits of human passion. You may well stand trembling beside that glorious junket-white belly, from which the golden oil of health is oozing, and quaff a hero's dram.

Elated with this success—it is evidently a taking day—you hurry off to Gowrie's Pot, as soon as proper respect has been paid to the dead monster, in the certainty that you are going to find a fish there too. Nor is your certainty ill-founded. Gowrie's Pot has the current on your side of the river and thus seems much easier to fish. You need cast only about fifteen yards, obliquely downstream, and the current immediately straightens out even the most amateur throw. Pleased with this, you cast about twenty-five yards, and this means that you are fishing almost directly downstream. The fish is there, just as you thought, and comes at you from below. You are in contact with your fly and haul back at him (or "strike") just as he begins his haul at you. "Got you, you beggar!" But the ghillie, who was standing high up on the bank, is running down to you exclaiming, "Too hard! Too hard!" just as he did before. The words are scarcely out of his mouth before the hook is out of the fish's, and here you are again with the fly lying on the bank at your feet.

This time the ghillie was right. The fish, coming from below you, took your hook in the hardest part of his mouth, the front of it, and you have simply pulled the hook away from him. It slipped out between hard palate and hard dentary. If you had possessed the self-control to *pay out* line when you felt him below you, you *might* have hooked him in the corner of the mouth, just as you hooked the fish which you never had a chance to strike at in Black Murdoch.

There. We fancy that we have given you a run for your money, and now it is time to go back to your hotel. Here comes the aged angler in the motor-car which is to take you home, and if we know anything about it he has got a bigger fish than you have or more of them. So don't hold up your trophy in triumph, the moment he comes into sight, or you will give him the opportunity of displaying his own superiority by means of affected humility. Go home quietly instead, and send off the fish by the earliest train, to the most influential person that you know.

Time to go Home

PART III

SHOOTING

A Certain Personage

§ 1

TYPES OF SHOOT

THERE are four kinds of shoot: the *Certain Personage*, *The Family*, the *Syndicate* and the *Farmer's Glory*. The first of these reckons to slay between one and three thousand pheasants on its best days and is exclusively ducal in its demeanour. A photograph is taken to commemorate each battue. In the middle of this photograph, which will be circulated to the press, the *Certain Personage* may be observed to be sitting astraddle like a benevolent toad. They got him bottled at luncheon, stationed a loyal and excellent shot on either side of him, and a useful man a little way behind. Thus no bird has been able to pass over the Personage without being subjected to frontal fire and enfilade on both flanks, as well as to the aimless discharges of the Personage from below. He is pleased with his shooting, pleased with his hostess (who stood beside him with

105

her pomeranian, just to the left of the loaders and in front of the camera men), pleased with the cherry brandy, and, in fact, vaguely pleased. The duke and duchess, his hosts, are sitting on either side of him to keep him upright, and that equerry behind has just dug him in the ribs to make him open his eyes for the photograph. The three famous marksmen who shot his birds for him so unobtrusively are those seedy and hatchet-faced gentlemen tucked away at the extreme end of the back row. For ten years now none of them has ever missed a bird, so they are all sent for at all the big shoots in order to back the Certain Personage and to keep the figures of the bag at a formidable level. Doomed as they are to a ceaseless round of discharging cartridges at the rate of a thousand a day, without any possibility of missing, and with only the briefest interlude for game pie and cherry brandy in the middle of the morning, these hired labourers are by now quite deaf, dyspeptic and disillusioned. They have rubber pads to guard their sore shoulders and gloves to guard their hands from being burned by the barrels of their guns, and they wear cotton wool in their ears. Nobody takes any notice of them once the shooting is over (and even then it is only the head keeper who troubles to put them at good stands, and this selfishly, so that he may himself show a good record), and they are perfectly sick of the whole business. One of them is interested in trains, one in boy scouts, and one in the design of life-boats, but here they are compelled to spend all their lives blowing off Messrs. Eley's cartridges and eating pies with bones in them.

All the other people in the photograph are colonels of Guards' Regiments, débutantes, dowagers and one or two rich Jews. The things in front are carcasses, and the object just beside the Hon. "Piggy" Plantaganet's right boot is a champagne bottle, empty.

The *Family Shoot* is a very different affair. Its proprietor was at Eton all right, just like all the people who shoot with the Certain Personage, but he has gone and had far too many children for his squire's estate, and he has made the mistake of sending them to Eton also. Impoverished by their education, persecuted by their ill-breeding and youthful spirits, he has been compelled to throw open his thousand acres of rough shooting to them and to such rapacious and inconsiderate acquaintances as they have made at school. The partridge rather than the pheasant is the quarry of this ménage, and it is pursued on foot in September to the accompaniment of loud shouts, practical jokes, badinage and ill-directed fusillades. Nor is it certain that the squire can safely spend the rest of the year in fiddling with the Home Farm, which is the darling of his heart. At every season of the year, and at every time of day, shots echo in every quarter of his estate and pellets spatter the leaves about his head, as one or another of his children assassinates a rook, a squirrel, a stray mallard, a rabbit or a little owl. One day some of his younger sons will fall on his head out of a dead tree, where they have been trying to take an eyas sparrow hawk, and the next he will be thrown upon his face by a rabbit wire in the park. The loose boxes in his stable are full of badgers, otters, hedgehogs, grass snakes, brown owls, fox cubs, ferrets and white mice. The rooms of his house are cluttered up with cartridge boxes, fishing rods, rabbit wires, long nets, clap nets, landing nets, tennis nets, purse nets, and butterfly nets. The conversation of his entire entourage (except of his wife, who went mad ten years ago and is now locked up with two trained nurses upstairs, believing herself to be a tufted duck) is confined to the habits of animals with their young: whether adders swallow them, woodcocks carry them, cuckoos lay them or put them there with their beaks. The whole of his family is never assembled at any one meal, owing to the fact that two or three of them are bound to have fallen into the lake, gone to watch a snipe drumming, or merely forgotten that they were hungry, and the result is that he does not quite know how many children he possesses, although he is generally able to distinguish his own brood from their friends, by marking down some family resemblance. The children all quarrel with each other incessantly, about who is to be allowed to take away the pair of Westley Richards for August, and who saw the Kestrel's nest first, and who has last used the gun oil and whether there is any water to have a bath. If you are a member of such a family, you are one of the luckiest men alive; but if you are not a member, and get invited to the Family Shoot, we can only say God Help You.

The *Syndicate* Shoot was begun in 1911 by a solicitor called Whistlefirst and a doctor called Beetle. As they were conscious of not being quite out of the top drawer, they were only too pleased when a retired colonel called Scarlett-Vermilion signified that it was his pleasure to honour them by joining in on payment of £25 a year, a sum which would reduce their own expenses of £100 each. Whistlefirst is still alive and pays his hundred pounds, but he is too old to shoot, and the syndicate can only send him a brace of pheasants now and then. Beetle took to his own drugs after being shot down twice by the colonel, and died in 1921. The colonel himself seceded in 1927 with half the territory, after quarrelling with all the new members of the syndicate, and died of apoplexy in 1928, after being accused (he was denying the accusation at the time) of shooting his seventh beater.

At present the syndicate consists of no less than eight guns, an awkward number, since it is impossible to be sure of a majority decision upon any point, there being usually four upon the one side and four upon the other. This difficulty is enhanced by the fact that the first four have not spoken to the second four since last January, when there was a row about who ought to have brought the coffee for luncheon. Major Pobble then accused Dr. Bones of having missed his turn for the pork pie twice running, while the ex-mayor stated that the Admiral had been using his cartridges since November. The Admiral said that it was the Major who missed the pork pie and the Major said that the Mayor had not paid for the cartridges. Young Pobble slapped the Mayor's nephew for saying that it was camp coffee. Dr. Bones's brother the accountant pointed out that pork pies were not the first thing the Major had missed, and the two Dog-worthies, both bank managers, were threatened with a horsewhipping for maintaining a silence which was deemed to be sarcastic.

There is only one keeper, an ex-convict called Murder, and he inclines alternately to either party, in accordance with the amount of tips received. Since he has no particular master, but only eight divided ones who are constantly bribing or cajoling him in their own interests against those of their comrades, Murder charges for twice the number of pheasants he rears and sells half that number to the heirs of Colonel Scarlett-Vermilion on the adjoining shoot. He also buys the cartridges, out of which he is able to make a good thing, entertains the local publican and friends to several good rabbit days, appropriates 25% of the fees supposed to be received by beaters, and earns a reasonable income by breaking dogs in the time which he ought to be devoting to his master's interests. The Syndicate shoots on every Saturday during the season, and never goes near its land during the other days of the week, thus making it easier for Murder to do what he pleases during six days out of the seven. The result is that each member of the Syndicate of eight has to pay a hundred pounds apiece, in order to enjoy rather less than half the sport that was enjoyed by Mr. Whistlefirst and Dr. Beetle for £200 between them.

Each member of the Syndicate is technically allowed to invite a guest, except during the three best days, but, as all the other members take the opportunity to insult that member by being rude to his guest, the option is rarely claimed. Another bar to invitations is that the guest has to be given some of the bag.

The sport enjoyed with a Syndicate shoot is fair. It is rare that members of a Syndicate should prove to be good marksmen, and so, when they do shoot each other, the coup is seldom fatal. Murder is for the same reason able to show a fair number of birds right up to the end of the season and, even if they are not actually brought to the ground, well, you saw them and had the pleasure of listening to the bang.

The *Farmer's Glory* is perhaps the happiest kind of shoot there is. In it there is no question of shooting at all. The farmers have just completed the heaviest and most nerve-wracking period of their year, the hay having been stacked for silage between thunderstorms and the corn harvested quite flat from the latest monsoon. They have done their job, divested themselves of heavy responsibilities, and now all they want is a little quiet relaxation. They like to see each other's farms.

Sauntering arm-in-arm across the warm September stubbles, exchanging reminiscences of the latest crisis and criticisms of the beasts which stray across their paths, the scattered bands wander across the farm in twos and threes. Sometimes a covey, caught between two converging parties, is raked fore and aft. A hare, fleeing from one jovial agriculturalist who has fired at it more in fun than anything else, runs through a gateway into the arms of two others who are weighing up the value of a rick. Here a bloodthirsty young fellow who badly wants to get a shot is making an enormous manœuvre to get round a covey of frenchmen; there a couple of sheep dogs are taking advantage of the general relaxation by chasing a rabbit. Under this tree is a battered motor-car bearing an homeric cheese and sausage rolls, under that one a party of mahogany men with ivory teeth are toasting each other in amber beer, while over there, on the skyline, four serious shooters are stalking the frenchmen from the opposite side to the bloodthirsty young fellow. All is sport, all is friendliness, all is far from businesslike; and yet it is a curious fact that these people seldom or never shoot one another, as the frowning members of the Syndicate do, observe none of the correct taboos, and consider (deluded fellows) that they have enjoyed a perfectly good day's outing when they have only slaughtered fifteen brace of partridges.

The Syndicate Shoot

III

§ 2

WE regret to say that the reasons for shooting on any scale at all, except for the farmer's simple reason of going out for a stroll on his neighbour's territory, are of such a psychological nature as to be perfectly unprintable. Suffice it to say that they are connected with an unsatisfactory married life.

Power of Locomotion

§3

CORRECT COSTUME

Just as the intellectual fisherman lays stress upon his hat because he keeps his cunning in it, so does the almost certifiable shooter lay stress upon his boots, because in them he keeps his only visible asset: the power of locomotion. Without this power he would be compelled to lie at home, a battered hulk, while with it he is enabled to plod from field to field, slaying wherever he goes.[1]

The Amateur Gentleman will find that various uniforms are common at various shoots (the plus-four being now almost universal at the Certain Personage's, while the Family goes out in running shorts or grey flannels, the Syndicate occasionally in breeches, and the Farmer's Glory in anything at all), but he will find that all shoots are distinguished by a galaxy of boots. The individuality of the shooter is expressed in these, as also is a certain amount of his superstition. Just as

[1] It is true that if he were blind he would also be unable to shoot very well, and it is a curious fact that shooters do, for this reason, devote special attention to their spectacles as well as to their boots. It is not that they wear spectacles, like everybody else, but that they often wear curious spectacles which are oblong, hexagonal, monocular or partly smoked. No doubt some homoepathic magic resides in this.

the Basuto woman is said to consume the flesh of the hippopotamus to make herself comely, so does the puny marksman wear farm labourer's boots to make himself walk far. The Cockney sportsman wears Newmarkets in order to give himself blue blood, and the Certain Personage wears spats with his knicker-bockers in order to reduce the blueness of his own. All this magic, however, is modified by climatic conditions and by the circumstances of the sport itself. It would be vain for the Cockney to colour his blood by wearing dancing pumps, court shoes or full dress spurs, since even the shortest grass would soon perish the former, while the latter would be apt to catch in roots. The ideal to be aimed at is hard wear and imperviousness to water, if possible as high as the knee, modified by whatever form of magic is most necessary to the Amateur Gentleman.

Full-length waders are splendid for snipe-shooting or walking in roots, but they are not so nice when you have to walk fifteen miles between drives or over stubble. Ordinary thick boots can be made to look knowing and workmanlike by purchasing a kind of canvas anklet which is strapped round the top of the boot and which increases its area of protection by at least one-sixteenth of an inch. All forms of walking shoe are quite hopeless, unless you are shooting with the Certain Personage, in which case it is likely that a carpet will be laid down for you from the motor-car to your next stand. Gum-boots, which keep out the wet very nicely, generate their own damp inside, and in any case are not considered *comme il faut*. Hunting boots are difficult to walk in, because of the great width between the instep and the heel. Field boots are very good, if you enjoy doing up laces. Strong boots worn with leather or canvas leggings can be successful, but the legging is apt to part company with the boot and sometimes to turn partly or totally back to front. Quarter-deck boots are too short. Divers' boots are too heavy. Sandals are eccentric. Moccasins and the footgear worn by the Pawnees of Sarawak are almost unobtainable.

Almost Unobtainable

Wrong Direction

§ 4

NECESSARY EXPENDITURE

THE old saying that up goes a guinea, bang goes a penny-halfpenny, and down comes three-and-six, is still a reasonable criterion to the price of a pheasant shoot in these islands, and it is also fairly true that the rent of a rough shoot may be reckoned at a shilling an acre. Between these extremes, of the important territory which is patrolled by eight gamekeepers and of the charming farm which is patrolled by none but yourself and the local poachers, there is a wide gamut of possible expenditure. But we take it that the Amateur Gentleman will not be fond of expenditure.

The next best job to buying or hiring a shoot is to get yourself invited to a shoot belonging to somebody else. This can be done in a number of ways, as for instance by saving the life of the proprietor in a shipwreck, by marrying his daughter, by discovering discreditable facts about his past life, by hiring a few acres of roots next door to his best drive, or by posing as a Certain Personage. There is a last but very difficult way, and that is to become such a proficient marksman that he will be delighted to have you in order to bolster up his bag.

The only other necessary expenditures are in guns, cartridges and tips. So far as guns are concerned, we have always found that it is not so much the price paid for them that does the damage as the identity of the person who is letting them off. A perfectly good pair of guns can be acquired second-hand for about twenty pounds—guns, that is to say, which discharge percussion rather than pin-fire cartridges and whose explosion is not actuated by visible hammers. The fact that they are not ejectors and possess no famous name upon their barrels can be concealed, with a little ingenuity, from all parties except the loader, and if you can take your gardener over to load for you the small leakage will make no difference at all. Such guns will kill quite as many birds as any others, provided that they are shot off in the correct direction. But it is advisable to buy a pair, even if you will generally need only one, because it will save you much face-saving on the rare occasions when you do get invited to a two-gun shoot. If you buy a single gun you will seldom be able to match it when your financial position improves, and then it will have to be discarded and a fresh pair bought.

The cost of cartridges is on a par with the cost of guns. They may be purchased with brass cases reaching almost to their tips and with the most exciting statistics as to the velocity of their powder. But if they are pointed in the wrong direction even the swiftest powder will be of no avail, while the tardiest black, if pointed in the right direction, will merely shroud the marksman and his victim in a cloud of smoke. Cartridges are like salmon flies. Use the kind in which you possess most confidence.

The matter of tips has always been a delicate one. They work out in actual practice on a very simple rule: gentlemen with incomes above £5,000 give 5/- or under, while gentlemen with incomes under £500 give £5 or over. The rich men have no need to impress the gamekeeper, so they can afford to be mean. The poor men are in desperate need of impressing the gamekeeper, so they are forced to be ridiculous. A bye-law or corollary can be added to this theorem, and this is that the amateur or bad shot gives more than the *habitué* or expert, because he feels a desire to propitiate his critics. The Amateur Gentleman will find that he can get away with a tip of £1 if he is invited to the Certain Personage later on in the season, while five or ten shillings will satisfy Murder, in the Syndicate, at almost any time.

Beaters, when shot, should be rewarded.

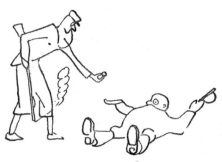

Rewarding Shot Beaters

Feeling Awkward

§ 5

TABOOS are apt to become transcendentalised, and to achieve an obscure objective existence of their own. The Children of Israel, we seem to recollect having heard somewhere, were forbidden to eat anything which chewed the cud and divided the hoof, because pigs were not good for their tummies in the desert. It is some time since the Children of Israel gave over their wanderings in that wilderness, but pork is still taboo. Another curious fact about etiquette is that when the moribund stage has been reached, the stage at which nobody remembers or understands the reason for the prohibition, any given set of rules is apt to be turned inside out and to be used for purposes quite opposite to those for which they were originally intended. The rule about pigs was started in order to distinguish between good and bad meats, but it is now used in order to distinguish between good and bad Jews.

When it was first discovered that to slay partridges in the breeding season tended to diminish the stock of these birds, a game law was introduced to protect the birds while they were breeding. This law is now used to protect the Amateur Gentleman from meeting people he would not like to meet—the lower classes, who kill birds out of season. It was noticed that people who left their guns leaning fully loaded against a wall were apt to bag an unwarrantably high percentage of their fellow-men, and so, in order to protect life, a tradition was started that arms should be unloaded before being piled. This tradition now exists mainly in order to distinguish the tyro from the habitual, both of whose lives would readily be sacrificed by every other member of the party.

Etiquette, in fact, begins as common sense, even if it ends up as aristocratic nonsense, and generally it deserves to be observed.

The chief etiquettes in shooting are connected with the lives of human beings and with the lives of those creatures which they intend to kill. Both lives are assumed to be valuable: that of the creature because if it is not alive you cannot kill it, and that of the human being for reasons much less logical and possibly quite fallacious.

The chief laws concerning human beings are as follows: Do not leave your loaded gun alone for any minute of the day, and especially not during luncheon.

Liquor is often consumed at luncheon during the colder months and in the resulting confusion it is perfectly easy for the wrong person to get shot. Do not at any time, whether you are walking, standing, joking or discussing its merits, allow the muzzle of your fowling piece to become directed at any living person. If you were to shoot him you would feel awkward. When negotiating any obstacle whatever, whether gate, hedge, ditch, rivulet, bank or railway line, take the cartridges right out of your gun. Putting on the safety catch is of no use at all, since you could knock it off as you fell. If you did fall on a slippery piece of timber and blew off your own foot, you would not only feel awkward, but look so. In closing the gun after you have loaded it, see that the muzzle is not only pointing at the ground, but also pointing at a bit of it which contains no feet or parts of recumbent shooters. Should either of the nipples be defective, you cannot fail to give the party a little surprise, but the foregoing precaution will at least save them a doctor's bill as well. Always be perfectly certain where your muzzle is pointing, and whether your piece is loaded. Confusion on either or both of these points has often resulted not only in obituary notices, but in grave discussion as to whether it was suicide or not. Every time that you unload your gun, say the Lord's Prayer through slowly, and look again to see whether you did unload it after all. Get yourself into the habit, however many miss-pulls it may initially cost you, of walking or standing with the safety catch on. Never vary this rule. When you have properly established the habit, the time taken in slipping the catch off subconsciously will help you in concentrating on the bird. Remember that briars and small twigs are able to pull a trigger and if, in extreme emergency, you happen to be moving in such stuff, cover the whole trigger guard with your right hand. Never put your finger inside the trigger guard, except in order to fire. Never fire at all unless you have clearly distinguished the *species*, and if possible the *sex* of your objective. Beaters are compelled by their trade to move about in bramble bushes,[1] so that a shot at unspecified objects in undergrowth is apt to produce surprising results, while, though it does not matter very much whether you assassinate a male or a female beater (there were female beaters during the war) your host may possibly have promulgated the doctrine that cocks only are to be shot. Keep a look-out in front of you when walking, and do not fire if approaching a road or a herd of cattle. Be chary of firing horizontally in any case. Divide your world into four quarters—in front, behind, and on either side—and never discharge except into the first or second. Do not even swing your gun through the other quarters, unless it be well overhead, in following from the first to the second. If, in spite of all these precautions, you happen to shoot a man, apologise; and if the man should happen to be your host you had better repeat the apology twice, go away quickly, and write a bread-and-butter letter.

The etiquettes concerned with the life of the bird or beast are mainly based upon their breeding seasons, the idea being that if you shoot a pair of partridges in May it is probable that you will have a dozen less partridges to shoot in September. This idea is for some reason not legally extended to hares and rabbits, although their meat is seldom worth eating before the middle of June. The Amateur Gentleman should therefore provide himself with a sporting calendar

[1]Dogs also are known to move in thickets.

which informs him clearly about the dates of the various close seasons, and he should adhere strictly to these seasons whenever he is not alone. He should remember that pheasants are not always cocks, and not always full grown, so that a chatter of four or five medium-sized buff birds out of a hedgerow as he is walking the wing in September, need not necessarily call for execution. The rule which lays down that you should make certain what you are shooting at is, indeed, excellent for creatures as well as for human beings. Young pheasants in September are rarely applauded, while little kudos is attached to the tame pigeon which flies directly over you without deviation of course. Finally it is well to remember that although Parliament has been kind enough to lay down for you the exact days upon which birds begin to mate, this does not preclude the exercise of a modicum of observation on your own account. The wild duck particularly is liable to disregard the rules of Parliament, and there is no need to shoot a couple which have paired simply because they are still in season.

In shooting foxes the Amateur Gentleman will make sure that he is alone or absolutely certain of his company. It is also well to ascertain that the fox is not being hunted. If, after shooting a fox, you should hear the faintly approaching toot of a horn, the best thing is to prop it up under a hedge in some natural position and to go away. Do not attempt to carry it away with you, as it is embarrassing to be followed home by twenty couple of hounds.

There are a certain number of etiquettes which are not connected with the preservation of life so much as with the preservation of equanimity. These are the taboos which have been furthest diverted by custom

123

from their original purposes. It was found, for instance, that a man who was continually boasting about his marksmanship became a thorn in the flesh to his fellow-shooters. If he was a good marksman, the fact was obvious, and his lesser companions hated him for it. The last thing they wanted was to be continually reminded of their inferiority. Whereas, if he was not a good marksman, it became unduly tedious to have to keep on admitting that he was. Besides, too much time was wasted in looking for alleged runners after he had clean missed. For these reasons a convention was established that nobody was to mention or emphasise his own skill. All thinking shooters realised that each one was really only interested in his own performances, and it was therefore better that each should be allowed to nourish his ego in silence rather than be compelled to pay attention to the clamouring egos of all the other guns. The bogus virtue of "modesty" was invented, in order to preserve the personal immodesty of each individual from the collective immodesties of his companions. It was a good idea while is lasted. It did not last long. The Frankenstein of modesty threw off the trammels of its creators, and achieved a separate and devastating existence of its own.

Nowadays modesty is used as a means of boasting, and the Amateur Gentleman will be wise to study its technique. Let him imagine himself posted in a deep valley at a pheasant shoot, the lowest of a long line of guns which stretches uphill beside the covert. Let a fine cock bird, already enormously high when it starts its course at the other end of this line, swing sideways over the guns in his direction and pass unscathed through the whole fusillade, presenting a more and more difficult shot to each gun as the valley dips below it. Let the Amateur Gentleman, in full view of all his thwarted companions, slay this bird with his first barrel, and let him then ask himself whether the natural reaction to such a feat would be to call out "Hoy!" or "What do you think of that, you beggars?" or to give a merry smile. Whether natural or not, none of these reactions can be considered correct. The correct reaction is to assume a false appearance of equanimity, to sneer or smirk mincingly down the nose, and to make no comment at all. This is called modesty, and it is a much more effective weapon for establishing superiority and galling one's companions than the old-fashioned shout of triumph could ever have been.

Again, it was originally discovered that the first thought of anybody who had discharged a fowling piece and seen the quarry fall to the ground, was: I hit it! If two or more persons discharged their pieces, they all experienced this conviction simultaneously. It was thus thought better that such a conviction should never be voiced, because, if it were voiced, there would be bound to be disagreement between the parties. It was established as a rule that no birds should ever be claimed, and shooters who have both blown off at the same object can still be seen growing purple in the face in the effort not to assert that it was they, and not the other man, who slew the victim.

The modern method, more subtle, is to press one's own birds upon other people, exclaiming: "Your bird, I think," in cases where it is quite obvious that the countrary is the case.

Other rules which exist for the general good nature of the community are those which deal with dogs. Do not take a dog when you are invited to a shoot without asking first whether you may, and do not ask for that permission unless you are certain that your dog will be a welcome addition to the shoot. Few things are more annoying for a host than to find that one of his guests has brought a white pekinese which is chasing field mice between the beaters and the guns. The main thing about a dog, as guest, is that it should be steady. It does not matter to your host whether it is a good working dog or a bad one, so long as it will only behave itself. If your dog possesses the accomplishment of sitting down behind you when told to do so, then you may take it with impunity: but you should not publicly ask it to work unless you are sure that it can. The guns on either side of you will be watching like lynxes for any opportunity of criticism, and the two great opportunities are the marksmanship of the master and the ability of the dog. Should you possess a dog which is able both to sit down and to retrieve, a rare combination, there are still some rules which ought to be obeyed. Do not allow the dog to retrieve birds which have been shot by your neighbour. He wants to impress the keeper by having as many birds lying at his feet as possible, when the man comes round to collect them, and he will naturally be infuriated to think that one of his birds is lying at your feet to do the same job. Do not offer your dog to hunt a neighbour's runner unless he is without a dog, or definitely asks for yours. However admirable her powers, do not take your bitch if she has rabies, distemper or an amorous disposition. Remember that love laughs at locksmiths, and reflect that no line of hard-bitten shooting men will enjoy to see their laboriously trained and proudly exhibited retrievers melting away unanimously in the mere pursuit of pleasure.

Finally, there are two shibboleths which relate to the method of slaughter. If a pheasant leaps out of a bramble bush at your feet, do not blow it to bits at a range of five yards. Such a course of action will render it quite valueless for the table, so that your host can neither sell it nor give it away to one of the guns. He will have to eat it himself, and the cook will probably give notice. The last rule is about sitting shots, and the Amateur Gentleman will be acquainted with it already. It raises such an interesting psychological problem, however, that it deserves a section to itself.

Mere Pursuit of Pleasure

Sport Unknown Among Butchers

§6

WHAT IS SPORT?

Pteryplegia, or the Art of Shooting Flying was written by
Mr. George Markland, who in 1726 was the first man
to recognise the possibility of slaying a pheasant on
the wing. Prior to this date the proper way to slay
a pheasant was when it was sitting down.

Sport is not the act of killing. Killing is a very
mere business, the prerogative of butchers and people
who want something to eat. It is practised by the
lower orders, aborigines and animals. Tigers kill, and
hawks do, but for the disgraceful purpose of eating
their victims. Sport is unknown among animals,
Aborigines, the lower orders and butchers. If sport
were merely the act of killing, it would be sport to
be a butcher or an Aborigine, and this is manifestly
not the case.

When you are throwing pebbles at a biscuit tin on
the seashore, and often hitting it, you will either go
farther away to make your shots or else set up a smaller

tin if such be available. You will handicap yourself. When the committee finds that the fourteenth hole was done by old Mr. Sloworm in two under bogey, they will lay out a new bunker or take the tee-box farther back. They will put difficulties in his way. When the magician finds that juggling with two balls has become so easy as to be second nature, he will either begin to juggle with four balls or give it up altogether, and anybody who has ever taken up knitting will know that no sooner had he mastered the plain and purl than he was anxious to match himself against a rope stitch or something like that.

It is this instinct, the instinct to back oneself against difficulties, that is the basis of all sports. The fisherman finds that it is relatively easy to catch trout on the worm, so he handicaps himself (increases the difficulty which has to be overcome) by determining to catch trout on a hook ornamented with a piece of rubber tube in the likeness of a worm. The slayer of foxes becomes bored by murdering them with a gun, so he expends eight thousand pounds a year in training dogs to do it in a much more complicated manner. The shooter, able to butcher any number of sitting rabbits by creeping up to them while they are feeding in the evening, stands up and waves his arms to make them run.

The greater the difficulty, the greater the pleasure in overcoming it. If there is no difficulty, there is no pleasure, and it is thus that difficulty or handicap has become the essence of sport, and that which distinguishes it from simple killing.

Retired colonels are apt to voice this truth unwittingly, when they say that a sitting shot is "unsporting" because it does not give the quarry a "sporting chance." What they mean is that the sitting shot is unsporting because it does not give them a sporting chance of missing (thus adding to their pleasure if they hit), but somehow or other the colonels have got the rôles mixed up, and for them the rabbit appears to be enjoying the sport which is laboriously offered to it by the colonel. Except for this slight confusion of personalities, the colonels are quite right.

Nearly all animals are beautiful and interesting while they are alive. This beauty is gravely diminished by death, because they are no longer able to move their beauty then, and motion is a great part of loveliness. Thus the young boy who shoots his first rabbit and stands holding it while the soft hazel eye of this quite harmless[1] and pleading herbivore moves through terror and agony to glaze: this boy, for that first time, realises that he has committed hideous murder, the sin against the Holy Ghost. A little chaffing by his seniors, the habit of a few more emulative slaughters, and a certain inherent beastliness still common to the human mind, will in the end render him impervious to such sensations—provided that he has made a good shot. When he murdered his first rabbit, possibly a sitting shot, he was horrified by the realisation that he had destroyed beauty. This horrible realisation will soon be dulled by custom, *provided that in destroying that beauty he can at the same time congratulate himself upon having created another beauty, the beautiful shot.*

This is what lies at the bottom of the taboo about sitting shots. It is a taboo created in order to save the shooter pain. If he destroys a sitting pheasant he has merely destroyed beauty, and some twinge of that

[1]Except to farmers.

young boy's emotion, which he once was, will return
to plague the inventor; but if he destroys it in its full
glory on the wing, he can smother this remorse under
the other beauty of his successful aim.

Slight Confusion of Identity

The Laird of That Ilk

§ 7

But the Amateur Gentleman will be anxious to set out upon his first real shot, and we are as anxious to have a good laugh while watching him. Let us put on our cloak of invisibility, therefore, and nascond ourselves behind his right shoulder, being careful to retain this strategic position throughout the day for fear of being shot while viewless.

Our host is the McInvert of McInvert, who has been persuaded to come back from Monte Carlo for a few weeks in order to settle his priceless collection of sea shells in their proper home at Castle McInvert. When he got back he found the editor of *Rivers in Britain* fishing his water and assumed that this gentleman must be Major Greene. Since he had managed to persuade the Laird of That Ilk to come back from Monte Carlo with him, however, for a last re-union

132

of the Ilk at some sort of Highland Games, this makes little or no difference. For the Laird has brought Major Greene over from the other coast for the day's shooting, under the impression that Major Greene is the friend of the nephew of his great-grandson, and neither of the aged Scotsmen is able to remember proper names for more than a few minutes in any case. Captain the Hon. " Piggy" Plantaganet is there, for his wife was born a member of the Ilk, and he has brought his friend the Master of the *Family Hounds*. How the Amateur Gentleman got invited remains a mystery. Perhaps the Laird has got him mixed up with the Ilk.

It is a bright day in December, and the McInvert's country is, it will be remembered, upon the East coast of Scotland. There are no moors in this particular part, no forests (so called because they are treeless), no Highland scenery of any sort. It is a shoot on the coastal plain, among arable farms and pasture with a few scattered coverts, much the same sort of mixed shoot as might be found in any part of the British Isles which is not devoted to grouse driving, duck flighting or the stalking of deer. Three Keepers are retained on these policies, two of whom are the sons of the third, and there are about three thousand acres which can be shot over in the long run—except that none of the McInvert's friends is now able to run for long, and only about a third of the territory gets visited at any one time.

It is a sunny day for the season of the year, and the party sets out in three motor-cars at ten o'clock in the morning for a distant rendez-vous understood only by the Keepers and the chauffeurs and partly by the McInvert. In the first car the McInvert is talking to the editor of *Rivers in Britain* about some people called Greene whom he met in Monte Carlo, and whether

they could be any relation, while the Laird of That Ilk
sits comatose beside the head keeper, upon whose lap
two spaniels are quietly being sick. In the second car
the Amateur Gentleman is squatting miserably between Captain Plantaganet and the Master of the
Family Pack, while the latter discuss, across him, such
subjects as (a) rotten bad shots; (b) social climbers and
their laughable inefficiency at all sports; (c) a man
called Booming who was horsewhipped for shooting
the Certain Personage in the left buttock while the
latter was patting his hostess's pomeranian; (d) dear
Diana's divorce, now absolute. In the third car Major
Greene is surreptitiously eating bismuth tablets
because of his tummy.

The cars arrive at the rendez-vous without mishap,
and the band of marksmen dismount with various
signs of rheumatism, ophthalmia, dyspepsia and cirr-
hosis of the liver. The Amateur Gentleman may take
this opportunity to sum them up. The Laird of That
Ilk, in his ninety-eighth year, is very sprightly considering, and can walk indefinitely all day so long as
he is able to sit down on a shooting stick for five
minutes in every hundred yards. He is dressed in the
cycling costume of the 'nineties, moderated by a plaid
shawl and a twa-snooted bonnet. The McInvert of
McInvert, who can scarcely be a day over seventy, is
handicapped by having a wooden leg, but gets along
pretty well. He is dressed in something which looks
suspiciously like the costume worn by American
athletes to play baseball in, only it is constructed out
of Harris tweed. The Master of the Family and
Captain Plantaganet are dressed in fashionable plus
fours, except that the M.F.H., who is a martyr to port,
got up in a bad temper this morning and put on odd
stockings. Captain Plantaganet, who is always dressed

by his valet, can suffer from no such mistake. Poor Major Greene is dressed in his fishing clothes, except for the waders. He is in a state of some confusion as to his own name, the name of his host, the locality in which he finds himself and the nature of the sport upon which he is now expected to embark. He has not shot since 1903, dislikes shooting, but suspects that he is going to be asked to shoot because they have taken away his fishing rod and lent him a gun.

The guns have sorted themselves out, the keepers have conversed together in incomprehensible tones, the dreary crew of hunched and drivelling peasants, who are the beaters (and they, unlike Captain Plantaganet, are dressed in old sacks, leather, string and brown paper) have been told where to go, a small silver cylinder has been produced by the McInvert, and everybody has selected a silver tally out of it with a number written thereon. The McInvert would have preferred to post his line himself, putting the Amateur Gentleman at one end of it (for everybody has by now detected his weakness by a certain shifty look in his eye) and himself at the other, but politeness to the rest of the guns dictates that lots should be drawn. The Amateur Gentleman's number is seven, so that when everybody moves up two places, as they do at the end of each drive, he will become completely baffled as to whether his number is now nine or two.

With a sprinkling of keepers and handymen leading dogs between them, the tottering line of marksmen is now led off to the stands. These have been marked with cleft sticks into which pieces of paper have been inserted, and on each piece of paper the number of the stand has been written in large, clear arabic numerals, so that even Captain Plantaganet's mathematics will not become confused. Captain Plantaganet, however, has wisely brought his valet to do the reckoning for him. Urged on by their attendants, supported by the stout arms of gamekeepers, conversing between their laboured breaths on the merits of steam trams, sea shells and other kindred topics, the upper classes are slowly shepherded into their positions, and more or less kept there, although they have a tendency to wander off in search of dogs, wild-flowers and things which they have dropped or left behind. The head keeper blows his whistle, and the Amateur Gentleman is in for it now.

He stands at the end of the line, a lonely figure. He has forgotten that the sun is ninety-three million miles away, and that the solar system itself is an insignificant pinprick in the isolation of the stars. He has forgotten that there are sixteen hundred million people in the world, all of whom will be dead in a hundred years: forgotten that even at this moment mothers are bearing children, old men dying, and young men being slain in wars. For him there is no longer any knowledge that *homo sapiens* has lasted for a hundred thousand years while he himself has lasted for about twenty. Man is born in sorrow, lives in sin and shortly dies in agony. He is surrounded by such men, all busy upon their own insignificant and pathetic fates, but such facts are not in his mind.

On the contrary, the whole circle of the enormous Universe is scooped, short-circuited inside him. He has gone broody.

Will one out of 1,600,000,000 shoot a partridge? Will twenty years out of one thousand million (the time it would take to reach the nearest star driving at full speed in your very fastest motor-car) distinguish themselves? Will the earth gape (weight 6,000,000 000,000,000,000 tons) to swallow him up if he makes a fool of himself, to hide him from the unbearable scorn of a dozen companions?

As a matter of fact, the answer to all these questions is No, but it is no good telling the Amateur Gentleman that. We can only leave him to stew in his own juice, to sweat with selfish fear, and to listen to the pounding of his tiny heart.

The first covey is coming over to the left, a baker's dozen of streaming meteors in brown feathers, and there one of them is altering its trajectory, growing downwards to the earth as Captain Plantaganet's column of faint smoke grows upwards to meet it. Another bird begins to roll itself up in a ball, with a tiny broken wing trailing behind it, as the noise of Captain Plantaganet's report reaches our ears. The second concussion arrives almost at the same moment, and then a third and a fourth with their attendant mushrooms of vertical smoke, so that it becomes obvious that Major Greene has fired also and that the second bird may have been his.

But there is no time for a study of the picturesque. The beaters are flapping their little flags and whistling, the birds are coming thick and fast. Here comes a whirr of wings, a noise of terror (for the Amateur Gentleman) that precedes the airy shrapnel by the very smallest margin, and a covey is directly overhead. We point our fowling piece at the middle of it and wildly tug the trigger—wildly, but uselessly, for we have left the safety catch on. By the time we have taken the gun from our shoulder, stared at it for a moment in wounded amazement, realised the situation, pushed the catch off and pushed it on again in the confusion, the covey is planing down with rigid wings two fields away. We watch them in an agony of remorse, watch them until the still wings all give

137

a flash together as the birds back-pedal on landing, and then another covey is overhead.

This time we make no mistake. Pointing the gun at the very thickest patch of them we somehow contrive to pull both triggers at once, and, practically stunned by the discharge, have the mortification of seeing the whole unharmed flotilla sailing sideways over the editor of *Rivers in Britain*, who scores a neat left and right while we are reeling with the shock.

The third opportunity is a single bird. We miss this and the editor kills it forty yards behind us.

It will not be until after the fifth or sixth covey, or perhaps at the second or third stand, that we shall actually begin to pray to God in so many words that no more birds may come over us. However much we pray, and almost as if in direct defiance of prayer, they will come over us more than ever, more than they go over anybody else, and we shall continue to miss them. "Over right!" the beaters will howl in despairing and accusing accents, while the whole line of guns will seem to our tortured imagination to be laughing heartily. Can it be the cartridges? Are we in front? Are we behind?

The fact is that we are taking the ridiculous business far too seriously, and poking in consequence, so that even if we picked our birds instead of browning them we should be equally unlikely to achieve distinction.

But there is no need to prolong the agony. Crawling from drive to drive, hoarsely inquiring of the next gun what he supposes our number ought to be, gruffly informing the keeper who comes round to collect them that No, we have no birds, we shall drag our shame along till luncheon. The Master of the Family Hounds will glare at us with contempt from the one side, while the editor sneers at us with contempt on the other. At luncheon we shall sit apart, tortured by our isolation if we are left alone and tortured by their condescension if the others offer us food. Occasionally, with glaring eyes which are not far from tears, and a strained voice previously unknown to us, we shall attempt a harsh laugh at some joke which has been made about steam trams. If we are so unbalanced by our sufferings as to have lost all control, we may even commit the fatal step of apologising for our shooting, blaming it on our spectacles or last year's cartridges or a new gun. Needless to say, this final degradation is to be avoided at all costs. It is to be pheasant after luncheon, and surely we shall be able to retrieve our reputation over them, for they are bigger birds?

Luncheon takes a long time. The older men are pleased to have a little warmth and comfort inside the keeper's cottage, while the middle-aged are glad to get a free go at the McInvert's sloe gin. All are merry because they have not proved to be the worst shot present, and the occasion seems ripe for celebration. Even Captain Plantaganet begins to sparkle and tells an anecdote about a chap who missed so badly that he missed his train home. This chap missed his train, see? Missed his birds, missed his train. He was a chap that missed. He missed his train home.

The Laird of That Ilk asks for this anecdote to be repeated, and points out, after some thought, that if it had been a steam tram Captain Plantaganet's friend would probably not have missed it, as they run more regularly. He adds that no doubt Captain Plantaganet's friend ought to have started sooner. The McInvert wants to know what Captain Plantaganet's friend's name was? Was it Greene, as he has heard of somebody of this name recently, who seems an odd fellow?

Major Greene says doubtfully that No, his name is Greene, not Captain Plantaganet's friend's. The McInvert looks at the editor of *Rivers in Britain* and says how odd that there should be two people of the name of Greene present, and now this friend of Captain Plantaganet's makes three: is this a record? The editor of *Rivers in Britain* tries to change the subject by claiming that the record Atlantic salmon weighed 79.38 lbs. The M.F.H. points out craftily that this was not, however, caught by Greene. Captain Plantaganet, confused by this publicity, says that his friend was not called Greene at all. It was a story. The editor says that the man who caught the salmon was called Henrik Henriksen. The Laird of That Ilk says that he does not see what this has got to do with steam trams; all agree. Captain Plantaganet repeats the story to make sure.

Luncheon is over at last, and the guests, exhausted by so much intellectual exercise and sloe gin, are hoisted out of their seats to resume the white man's burden. The Amateur Gentleman, perfectly sober and now suffering from nervous indigestion, goes to his gun in a tremble between terror and despair.

The afternoon's pheasants are located in three contiguous spinneys which can be taken in three drives, as it is realised by the head keeper that his gentlemen will not be able to walk farther than the half-mile which will be necessary to get to these stands. The tallies are drawn again, as everybody except Captain Plantaganet's valet has forgotten his number, and the procession is again formed in a kind of wandering crocodile which stretches for several hundred yards between the impatient M.F.H. and the Laird of That Ilk, who is hobbling along arm in arm with the McInvert, the two of them practically supported by the latter's wooden leg. A few camp followers pace deferentially behind, carrying shawls, stools, ear-trumpets, umbrellas and wheeling a bath-chair in case of emergencies.

The Amateur Gentleman has of course been un-fortunate enough to draw the number of the very best stand, and to be situated between the M.F.H. and Captain Plantaganet. These take up their positions with quiet assurance, point their guns in the air and squint along them in a professional manner, cause their extremely expensive dogs to sit down behind them without any bother and exchange jocular gestures through the Amateur Gentleman, as if he were a television set. Only he would be rather a cheap set. The stand is situated beside a high railway em-bankment which borders the covert in which the pheasants lie. The birds, driven out of their plantation, will cross the railway line to give the guns some splendid high shots as they stand at the bottom of the embankment, and the guns themselves are ranged two deep. The head keeper is stationed behind the Amateur Gentleman to the left, in order to improve the statistics of the bag, and his host is situated behind him on the right, apparently in order to make certain that his per-formances can be officially observed.

There is a long wait, during which his nerve may steady itself if it can, or go further to pieces in the almost certain event that it can't, and then, without any preliminary hullabaloo, the birds begin to come. The embankment has muffled the tapping, shouting and whistling of the bowed and ragged beaters, so that the first birds arrive as a horrible surprise, a series of Chinese dragons with long pointed tails (far too long for the marksman, who reflects, according to the old adage, how many thousands of pheasants he would have killed if only their heads had been in their tails) which stream over like lordly and unattainable fire- works at a height apparently incalculable. On the other side of the embankment they are rising out of the last border of their plantation like a *feu de joie*, six or seven at a time, and they sail over on this side too high to be audible, a snowstorm of floating pterodactyls, silent crucifixes passing like a plague.

Ils ne passeront pas! is the watchword at the Amateur Gentleman's salient, as he directs his muzzle vertically into the air and fires upward at the streaming bellies, which seem only just in range as they are crossing the zenith. But they do pass. Miraculously, humiliatingly unscathed, they trail across the sky immediately above his head, to be slain behind him by the head keeper or on either side by Captain Plantaganet and the M.F.H. The growing pile of cartridges about his feet is begin- ning to become a testimony and an accusation. Each empty case that he adds to it is as bad as a poem by Tennyson about the days that are no more, and he adds them continuously, two at a time. Finally, when the drive is over, he will be able to make a doubtful claim to two birds: one of which was shared between him and Captain Plantaganet, while the other, wriggling in the air, went on to be slain by the keeper. At the other two stands, which are less important, his own position will have been a less favourable one and he will not have added to his total.

Sixty-five cartridges and two birds. On the drive home there will be nothing for it but silence, and at dinner that evening he will probably take too much to drink. In any case he will flee from Castle McInvert at the earliest opportunity, praying neurotically that none of his companions may ever see his face again.

The Amateur Gentleman may possibly save himself from the madhouse if he will accept one final word of advice. Should his first shoot really prove to be as bad as the one we have described, let him go into a corner quietly by himself, sit down in a comfortable chair, close his eyes and place his fingertips together. There, in solitude and silence, let him compose his mind for five minutes, by means of prayer or counting sheep, and at the end of that time let him reflect upon these last immutable truths:

1. As a matter of fact the M.F.H. was not scowling at him with contempt. He was only scowling because of his liver, and never saw the Amateur Gentleman at all.

2. The editor was not sneering. He was smiling at the Amateur Gentleman with the friendliest feelings, because he was shooting well himself.

3. Everybody has shot like this once.

4. The sun is still ninety-three million miles away.

5. To-morrow is a new day.

APPENDIX

APPENDIX A

(*T. H. White's Method*)

PURCHASE an 8/0 hook, a reel of red silk (you will need it all), a reel of silver tinsel, a hen pheasant's tail feather, a dyed cock's hackle feather, a lump of beeswax, a bottle of spirit gum and a special vice for holding the fly while it is tied.

If you were intending to tie a trout fly, this vice will be suitable for holding salmon lures: if a salmon lure, it will be suitable for trout flies. In either case buy another of the other.

Place the hook in the vice, thus:

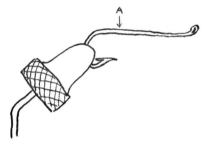

and select about two yards of the red silk off the reel. Tie a Granny-Knot in this and attach it to the hook at the point marked A. Attempt to wind it round the shank of the hook in order to make a foundation for the tag. It will be found that the knot revolves quite freely about the shank, thus making it impossible to make a foundation for the tag.

Take the beeswax and make the shank sticky, or adopt any other means which seem reasonable to you, but in any case endeavour to do something which looks like this:

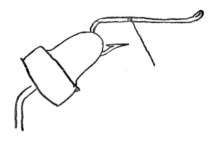

It will probably look like this:

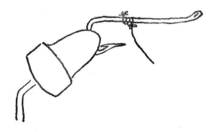

Now reflect that you have forgotten to buy any-thing suitable for the tag. Cut off a few strands of the pheasant feather, which will have to do instead, and attach them thus:

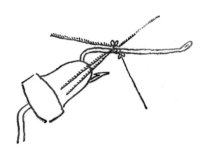

It will be found that they also revolve freely about the shank of the hook, but go on, do something, can't you? Well, wind some more of the silk round them.

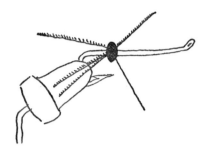

Now cut off two yards of the silver tinsel, at the same time attaching the end of the red silk to the pair of forceps which you have forgotten to buy and allowing the same to dangle beneath the hook. Tie the end of the tinsel to the now growing bundle of red silk, thus:

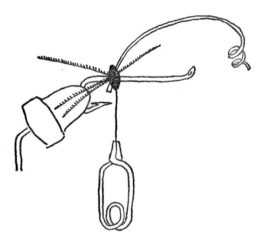

and wind the tinsel round the shank of the hook until you reach the eye.

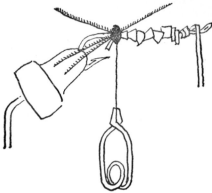

You will observe that your silk is at one end of the hook and your tinsel at the other. Your object is to bind the tinsel with the silk. The best solution is to abandon the first two yards of silk, with forceps attached, and to start again with a new Granny-Knot in a fresh two yards of silk at the eye end.

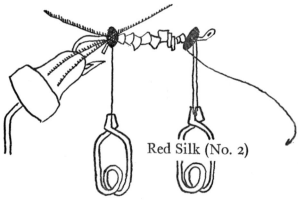

Red Silk (No. 2)

Sit down now for a bit of a rest, and work out what ought to be the next thing. (Remember to keep hold of Red Silk No. 2 as you sit down, or an unusual position will result). The next thing ought to be the hackle.

Take the hackle feather, pull off its fluff, and attach to the hook end, thus:

150

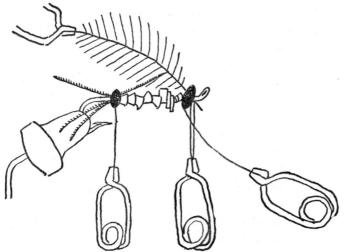

Wind the hackle feather (if it does not also revolve) round the hook end until there is no more to wind and then reflect that you have not prepared your wing feathers. While you are attending to the latter, the lure will have to be left under forceps in the following position:

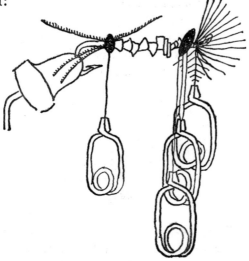

The wing feathers are prepared by splitting a section of the pheasant's tail feather down the middle

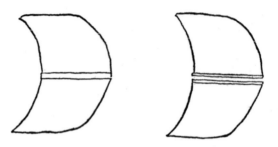

and by tying another piece of thread with a Granny-Knot round each sail, thus:

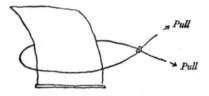

The resulting wings will be found to present the following appearance in each case:

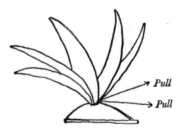

When these have been prepared they should be attached to the hook end of the shank above the turns of red silk, one on either side of the shank, and the whole should be bound in with silk, to make the completed fly:

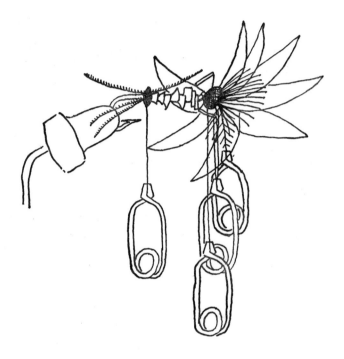

This fly should be finished off with a liberal dressing of spirit gum, as it is impossible to understand any of the knots or whip-finishes which are applied to flies, and should be allowed to set. If preferred, the forceps may then be neatly cut off with a pair of scissors: but this is liable to weaken the construction. It is the simplest form of sunk fly now used.

APPENDIX B

THE commonest casts are the Tree Cast (Fig. 1), the
Knot Cast (Fig. 2), and the Whip Cast (Fig. 3). These
casts need little or no description.

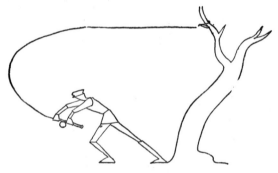

Fig. 1

Fig. 2

Fig. 3

There are, however, a certain number of more complicated casts, such as the Lasso, which is performed in two movements by throwing the line perpendicularly into the air and allowing it to fall in spirals about the angler (Figs. 4 and 5), and the Ear or Skull Cast, which is seldom forgotten once it has been achieved (Fig. 6).

Fig. 4

Fig. 5

Fig. 6

APPENDIX C

ALL good things come to an end, and even the most enthusiastic Amateur may one day become a Professional, with a grey beard like our own himself. Old age has a curious effect upon people, taking many spiritual veils away from the eyes which it has at the same time begun to cover with a more physical dark. Hunting may become a weariness to old bones, shooting a supererogatory dealing of death for one who is himself within its shadow. Even salmon fishing loses half its charm when the tired sportsman realises that he will catch the fish which are there, but not those which aren't. Trout fishing remains. The acme of sport, the final distillation of beauty: it alone can be pursued into the very jaws of death, into the mouth of hell.

In trout fishing at its highest there is no question of killing at all. The rod, line and gut cast are carried as a concession to public opinion, and also as gear which can be used as hobbies during winter months; when they are taken to bits, re-bound, re-varnished, dried, dressed and tied up in convenient bundles. They are not for use. The working part of the gear is comprised by the fly-tying materials and a small sort of butterfly net.

The true authority on trout goes down to the river with his little net, and walks along the bank until he has observed some fly upon the water. He then walks beside this fly for a mile or two, until it is accessible

157

to his net, and fishes it out as best he may, with or without falling in. He sits down on the bank with his magnifying-glass, and endeavours to establish the fly's adherence to the broad principles of the *plecoptera*, the *trichoptera* or the *ephemeridæ*. If of the latter kind he then begins to count the number of its wings and *setæ*, and finally stows it away in one of the numerous little bottles containing river water, alcohol, formalin, menthol or cyanide in plaster of paris which he carries about his person. It is now time to hurry back to the spot at which he left his fly-tying materials, and to construct (see Appendix A) an exact copy of the fly which he found upon the water. It may be necessary to go home for the only appropriate hackle, which he happens to have left behind, but this inconvenience may be overcome by hiring a small van which can convey *all* his materials to the river side.

When the fly has been tied on a three-o hook, the angler returns to the water at the point where he first saw the living insect and fits together the joints of his rod. He attaches the reel, pulls the line through the rings, ties on a 4x cast, knots the artificial fly to the end of it, and draws the rod back to cast. He then sees a grannom on the water (*Brachycentrus subnubilis*), while the fly which he has constructed is a good imitation of *ephemerella ignita*. He puts down the rod, searches for his fly-net, and repeats the process from the start. As there are thirty genera of the *trichoptera* alone, this exercise may be performed *ad infinitum* throughout the year. All informed trout fishing may thus be called a genuinely *constructive* sport.